THE AAM GUIDE TO COLLECTIONS PLANNING

James B. Gardner and
Elizabeth E. Merritt

AMERICAN ASSOCIATION OF MUSEUMS

PROFESSIONAL
EDUCATION SERIES

©2004 American Association of Museums
1575 Eye St. N.W., Suite 400, Washington, DC 20005

The essays in this publication are based on discussions at the Colloquium on
Collections Planning organized by AAM and the National Museum of American
History, Smithsonian Institution, Nov. 15-16, 2002, Washington, D.C.

On the cover (detail): *Knobbed Whelks (Busycon carica)*. Photo by Rosamond
Purcell. Originally published in *A Long Look at Nature: The North Carolina State
Museum of Natural Sciences* by Margaret Martin, Chapel Hill: University of North
Carolina Press, 2001.

Design: LevineRiederer Design

Library of Congress Cataloging-in-Publication Data

The AAM guide to collections planning.
    p. cm.
  Includes bibliographical references and index.
  ISBN 0-931201-88-8
  1. Museums--Collection management--United States. 2. Museums--United
States--Planning. 3. Museums--United States--Management. I. Sullivan, Martin
E. II. Gardner, James B., 1950- III. Merritt, Elizabeth E. IV. American Association
of Museums.

  AM133.A22 2004
  069'.5--dc22

                                2004002443

THE AAM GUIDE TO
COLLECTIONS PLANNING

TABLE OF CONTENTS

ACKNOWLEDGEMENTS

This publication distills the experience and wisdom of many people. We are fortunate to have had the opportunity to learn from their experiences of trying to implement collections planning at their institutions.

Our thanks go to Jane Lusaka, our editor at AAM, for helping us give voice to these experiences.

Much of our thinking on this topic is based on the discussions during the National Collections Planning Colloquium, developed by AAM in collaboration with the National Museum of National History and held at the S. Dillon Ripley Center of the Smithsonian Institution in November, 2002. Colloquium participants—80 people representing 36 institutions, as well as 11 facilitators—worked very hard for two days to discuss the issues at the heart of this book. Participants are listed in full in appendix G.

We are indebted to Lynne Poirier-Wilson, who led NMNH's initial discussions prior to the colloquium, and to Heather Berry of AAM, who conducted background research. We thank Kate Henderson of NMAH for organizing the colloquium logistics and Victoria Garvin of AAM for her vital role in shaping the content. Without their efforts the colloquium would not have been possible.

We thank the following people for allowing themselves to be drafted onto session panels at museum association meetings where we explored this topic: Patricia Ainslie, Claire Davis, Christine Flanagan, James Fogerty, Moya Hansen, Melissa Marsh Heaver, Pete Lesher, Jane MacKnight, Janet Rassweiler, and Sheila Riley.

We particularly wish to thank the staff of museums that have allowed us to use extracts from their collections plans in this publication: Chesapeake Bay Maritime Museum, Cincinnati Museum Center, Colorado Historical Society, Kalamazoo Valley Museum, Minnesota Museum of American Art, Morris Arboretum of the University of Pennsylvania, the Portland Museum of Art, the State Historical Society of Iowa, The Children's Museum of Indianapolis, The Mariners' Museum, and the Museum of International Folk Art.

And finally, we thank the current and recent members of the Accreditation Commission who inspired consideration of this issue at AAM, and whose thoughtful discussions regarding collections stewardship laid the groundwork for our thinking: Stuart Ashman, Betsy Bennett, Leslie Bowman, Lonnie Bunch, Kinshasha Holman Conwill, Irene Hirano, Jesse Otto Hite, Katherine Kane, Thomas Livesay, Freda Nicholson, James Peterson, Katharine Lee Reid, James Welu, and Arthur Wolf. We are particularly grateful to Martin Sullivan, current chair of the Commission, who contributed the introduction to this volume. ■

Elizabeth E. Merritt
James Gardner

INTRODUCTION:
COLLECTIONS STEWARDSHIP AND
COLLECTIONS PLANNING

*By Martin Sullivan, Chair, AAM Accreditation Commission,
and Executive Director, Historic St. Mary's City, St. Mary's City, Md.*

C ollections planning has begun to emerge as an essential "best practice" for museums, perhaps with greater urgency now that so many institutions are confronted by sharply reduced financial resources. As a member of the AAM Accreditation Commission for the past six years, I have examined collections plans and practices in more than 500 museums—zoos, aquariums, historic sites, children's museums, science centers, art museums, and every other kind of collection-based institution.

What impressions emerge from seeing the inner workings of so many places? Overwhelmingly, that America's museums try their very best to document, care for, and interpret their collections. Collectively, we hold an amazing number of significant objects and specimens worthy of preservation and interpretation. And though adequate money and staffing admittedly are problems at most places, I have to marvel at the hard work and creativity that my colleagues bring to the challenge of improving collections stewardship.

But even the most dedicated institutions can accumulate serious problems over time. In recent years, more than one-fourth of the Accreditation Commission's tabling actions—i.e., postponing the final decision about accreditation—have cited inadequacies in collections stewardship. The causes may include low levels of documentation, poor storage conditions, critical conservation needs, collections that appear unrelated to the museum's mission, or gaps in procedures and policies. Often, tabling actions that involve the care and management of collections also identify deficiencies in an institution's long-range planning process: plans that aren't sufficiently comprehensive or current, or that do not appear to give adequate priority to stewardship responsibilities.

When the Accreditation Commission votes to table, the message we want to send is not that the museum in question is unworthy, but rather that a focused and energetic effort may be the best way for that museum to improve its practices and demonstrate a track of steady progress. I am consistently impressed by the ways museums use their tabling periods to make impressive and lasting improvements in their stewardship and service.

Visiting committee members and accreditation commissioners rely on our own experiences and awareness of trends in the field to articulate the standards and best practices that go hand-in-hand with being accreditable. To help our colleagues understand how the commission interprets these evolving standards and practices, we've published a series of "expectations" documents that are accessible online at www.aam-us.org.

The commission's *Expectations Regarding Collections Stewardship*, approved in June 2001, states that museums need to plan intelligently as they acquire and assume responsibility for new materials, ideally within the framework of a carefully developed collections plan. An accreditable museum must demonstrate that its "collections and/or tangible objects are appropriate for its mission" and that the mission statement drives its policies, procedures, and practices regarding the development and use of those collections. Perhaps this is self-evident, but some museums continue to hold on to older collection materials that aren't pertinent to their current mission, or are tempted to acquire objects for reasons other than their significance to the mission.

As part of the accreditation review of collections management procedures, a further expectation is that "regular assessment of, and planning for, collection needs (development, conservation, risk management, etc.) takes place and sufficient financial and human resources are allocated for collections stewardship." Equally important, the institution must be able to demonstrate that "considerations regarding future collecting activities are incorporated into institutional plans and other appropriate policy documents."

At present, AAM accreditation standards do not require the submission of a specific collections plan; instead they stress the importance of collections management policies and procedures and evidence of a current institution-wide strategic or long-range plan. Still, I think the benefits of attempting to articulate a collections plan are becoming much clearer to our field. As this book indicates, much can be gained by looking closely at internal collection needs, gaps, and priorities, as well as at opportunities to collaborate with other institutions with similar missions. The most cogent collecting plans, in my mind, are those that embrace not only staff interests and expertise but also opportunities to better serve our audiences and communities.

This book and the November 2002 National Collections Planning Colloquium (organized by AAM and the Smithsonian's National Museum of American History) on which it is based are important steps in an ongoing field-wide conversation that is sure to engage all of us. On behalf of the Accreditation Commission, I express our gratitude to James Gardner at the National Museum of American History and AAM's own Elizabeth Merritt for their superb leadership in launching this conversation. ■

BUILDING THE INTELLECTUAL FRAMEWORK

By James B. Gardner, Associate Director for Curatorial Affairs,
National Museum of American History, Behring Center,
Smithsonian Institution, Washington, D.C.

C ollections planning begins with an intellectual framework that states the rationale for, or theory of, the collections and collecting. This is the most critical piece of collections planning—the compelling vision that defines your museum's unique role and provides the context for making decisions about the future of the collections. It also is the most difficult piece of the plan to develop, requiring a long, hard look at where the museum is going.

Why Do You Need an Intellectual Framework?

Put simply, an intellectual framework is the key to establishing intellectual control over the museum's collections. However, rather than working within a clearly established vision for the entire collection, museums too often rely on relatively autonomous curators. Certainly, individual curators at many museums have intellectual control—their knowledge of the collections is truly impressive, and they always have collecting initiatives underway. But they often pursue rather idiosyncratic goals, building on their predecessors' interests and work and adding depth and new topics but in isolation from other staff and the institution's larger goals. That is not the same as the museum having intellectual control; the parts don't always add up to a whole. The "plans" at such museums are little more than unit-by-unit lists identifying what is already in the collections and a few priority collecting targets.

How can a museum make the right choices if it doesn't have a larger vision of what the collections should be? Every museum should have a clear sense of what it aspires to be and how it expects to shape and develop its collections as a whole. An intellectual framework provides that big picture—defining, limiting, expanding, and clarifying what the museum collects within the context of its overall mission and goals.

For some institutions, establishing intellectual control provides the basis for more disciplined collecting during times of shrinking resources. For others, it is essential for assessing collections and focusing resources on new collecting initiatives. But regardless of the context, the end result is the same—moving the institution from ad hoc, idiosyncratic collecting to strategic, integrated collecting; from simply building the collections to shaping them; from asking "does it fit within the collections?" to asking "what should be in the collections?"

Getting Started

As with any planning effort, the process of developing an intellectual framework is often as critical as the end product; the process provides the vehicle for buy-in by staff, governing authority, and others. While curatorial staff may see the intellectual framework as their sole property and responsibility, the success of the larger collections planning initiative rests on getting broad support and incorporating diverse points of view. It is essential that the process encompass the full range of stakeholders—not only the governing authority and staff but museum members, audiences, communities, and outside scholars and specialists. Whether the work proceeds from the bottom-up, the top-down, or some combination of the two depends on the culture of the particular institution. But in the final analysis success will depend on whether the process is broadly inclusive.

The actual development of the framework begins with the museum's mission statement. While your mission statement is not likely to provide a clear enough vision for the collection in and of itself, it should state the role of collections in fulfilling the institution's mission and usually establishes basic parameters of place, time, and subject. The intellectual framework builds on that, "interpreting" the mission and providing a bridge from the mission to the collections and collecting.

Where you go from there depends on such variables as your museum's discipline, function, and other defining characteristics. There is no model or formula that fits all; the framework should take whatever form works for your institution. It can consist of statements or parameters, or it can pose questions to frame the collecting effort. The Kalamazoo Valley Museum[1], for example, combines both approaches, with themes tied to questions, such as "Family: who are we?" It is easier to say what the framework should not try to do: it should not be an assessment of the collections and should not include such criteria as provenance or value or address policies and procedures. It should, simply, establish a vision for the collections. As such, it should be detailed enough to guide collecting but not too restrictive or confining. It should provide focus but with enough flexibility to allow for collecting directions that respond to new scholarship and evolving institutional goals.

Different museums have used different formats and approaches successfully. The Kalamazoo Valley Museum adopted a matrix approach that essentially overlays four different frameworks—the themes mentioned above as well as topics, time period, and object type. The Colorado Historical Society's framework is more straightforward—six broad themes or subjects, such as cultural diversity. The Chesapeake Bay Maritime Museum provides thematic statements, for example, "People and the Bay: From early settlement to today, the natural environment of the Bay has attracted a diverse population that has given shape to distinctive settlement patterns, communities, and cultures." Art museums tend to structure frameworks around cultural groupings, as does the Lowe Art Museum, or artistic medium, as does the Portland Museum of Art.

What Are the Issues?

Developing an intellectual framework is hard work, and there may be resistance within your institution to the fundamental premise of a framework driven by ideas and concepts. Critics will question whether, if it is "intellectual" in that sense, a framework can have any real bearing on the material culture, the things the museum collects. Someone is bound to propose that it might make more sense to create a vision that grows out of the collections and builds on what you have rather than on abstract concepts. Someone else will ask whether you should factor in the vision of founding collectors, as the North Carolina Museum of Art and the Kalamazoo Valley Museum have done. In the final analysis, while a framework must connect to the real world of the museum and the collections, it should not be restricted by the past. It is by definition a vision of what the collections should be, not what they have been or are and, once established, becomes the basis for assessing the collections' strengths and weaknesses.

Museums developing intellectual frameworks have to grapple with tensions between:

■ *Collecting goals and interpretive goals*: Is your museum's collecting driven largely by exhibition and program goals or are there separate and distinct collecting goals? Should you develop collections around exhibit plans, or is that too limiting? Do you have the responsibility and the resources to build collections for documentary or research purposes? Answering such questions is critical; for example, a research collection must be more comprehensive than one used largely for exhibition or interpretation, which can rely on more representative, selective objects.

How you answer those questions will depend on your intended audiences. For The Children's Museum of Indianapolis that means children and families, for whom the museum develops "extraordinary learning experiences." The museum thus collects artifacts and specimens that are "powerful storytellers" for use in exhibitions and programs, and its intellectual framework is essentially its interpretive plan. On the other hand, the State Historical Society of Iowa claims several audiences—not just museum visitors but researchers, genealogists, government agencies, historic preservationists, and the society's members and subscribers—which has led to a different kind of vision and a more comprehensive collecting approach. And the Cincinnati Museum Center defines the audiences for its archeological collections not in terms of museum visitors but as "internal" researchers and educators and "external" researchers and educators, including users from colleges and universities, nonprofit institutions, government agencies, consulting firms, corporations, and the news media. Accordingly, the museum's focus is largely on developing a research collection in the field of archaeology.

■ *New directions and legacy collections:* How will the new intellectual framework deal with legacy collections? A history museum, for example, may embrace new historical scholarship that challenges the rationale for some of its current collections. Should the museum continue to build long-standing collections of record, or should it shift to new areas that reflect current scholarship and new interpretive plans? What happens to taxonomic/synoptic collecting traditions when the museum adopts a thematically focused framework? Should new collecting initiatives take priority over stewardship of historical collections? Should the priority be the long-term legacy of the collections or more current interpretive needs and interests? Are the two compatible or at odds? In the final analysis, do you develop a framework that builds on your strengths or that strengthens new areas? The Portland Museum of Art's "Theory of the Collection" proposes both with a well-defined collections vision and identification of "selected areas of excellence" that fall outside that vision.

■ *Current needs and future needs:* When setting priorities, how do you balance "now" and the "long term"? A framework that is too "of the moment" may not serve the best interests of the museum over time, distracting it with the trendy at the expense of larger collections responsibilities. The Colorado Historical Society plan recognizes this tension, acknowledging, for example, the problems of defining "cultural diversity" but arguing that it must still be a priority.

■ *Passive collecting and planned collecting:* Some curators believe that museums should not take the lead but should first step back and wait to see what the public values and saves. They argue that museums need distance and time to determine what to collect and should not try to leap ahead with proactive planning. But will we then run the risk of losing opportunities in our fast changing and increasingly disposable world? Plans such as that under development by the National Museum of American History try to allow for both serendipitous acquisitions and carefully worked-out documentation strategies.

■ *Institutional goals and collective responsibilities:* Should a collections vision focus solely on the institution or can it establish a framework for collaborative collecting? Can a vision be collective and the responsibility shared? For example, most museums are interested in addressing issues of diversity, but is it realistic for all to think they can develop those collections? What happens when we start competing for scarce objects? When regional and national institutions compete with local ones? Should every museum take this topic on? If a museum is coming to the subject late, should it try to catch up, or can its collections plan acknowledge the plans developed by other institutions? How might a museum's collections vision address that? For models, see the plans of the Lowe Art Museum and the State Historical Society of Iowa, each of which establishes a vision for its collections within the context of a conscious assessment of collecting at other institutions. Or consider the Kalamazoo Valley Museum's plan, which explicitly limits its collecting within the context of collections at institutions in a 50-mile radius.

The Framework and Beyond

However you address the issues mentioned above, your goal should be a framework that is clear and understandable. The goal is not to reflect the current scholarship and jargon but to provide a persuasive argument, to establish a single vision. Keep it simple; don't overload the framework with scholarly digressions. What it will look like in terms of format is not important; your framework can be a discreet section of your plan, or it can be merged with the other elements identified in "Writing a Collections Plan." The important thing is to establish a clear vision for moving forward with planning—for assessing and revaluing objects, making difficult decisions to deaccession, and initiating new directions.

Notes

1. Some of the plans cited in this chapter are excerpted in appendix A; all are available from the AAM Information Center (see appendix C). ∎

WRITING THE COLLECTIONS PLAN

By Elizabeth E. Merritt, Director, Museum Advancement & Excellence,
American Association of Museums

his chapter outlines the elements of a collections plan, explor-
ing for each:

- its purpose
- the role it plays in the planning process
- typical content

Not all plans contain all the elements described here, and there is no standard for what goes in which sections, the names of the sections, or their
order of appearance. This chapter, however, creates a model of all the elements that can contribute to a successful plan and suggests some ways they
might be arranged. See figure 1 for a sample outline for a collections plan,
and assess what content and format will work best for your museum.

Use this chapter in conjunction with appendix A, which includes extracts
from sample collections plans. (Complete copies of these and other plans
are available to AAM institutional member museums from the AAM
Information Center.) Remember that the planning document is just a
bunch of paper—a good way of capturing and transmitting information,
but only useful if it is the result of a thoughtful planning process. Many
of the elements discussed here are created primarily as a means of driving
that process. For that reason, this chapter discusses how and why to write
each element, as well as what should be included.

Here are some issues to think about before addressing the content and format of the collections plan:

Context

The collections plan is one in a series of documents that guide the museum's decision-making. These may include:

- mission statement (statement of purpose)
- vision statement
- strategic plan (long-range plan, institutional plan)
- interpretive plan
- site/building master plan
- financial plan
- fund-raising/development plan

The mission statement is the first and most fundamental of these. One of the three basic duties of a nonprofit trustee is the *duty of loyalty*—the legal obligation to guide the organization's activities to fulfill the mission. However, the mission statement is usually broad enough to encompass many, many choices. The remaining planning documents function as a series of filters, creating logical structures that narrow those choices and providing guidance that is specific enough to help reasonable people make a decision. For example, the strategic plan identifies specific goals, strategies, and action steps, all concordant with the mission, that the museum will pursue over a short period (usually about one to six years). A museum's strategic plan is comprehensive, addressing the most important issues facing the museum in all areas—marketing, programs, building improvements, finances, etc. Many museums have additional plans that address these areas in more detail. The collections plan provides this level of detail for collections development. It filters the potential choices regarding acquisitions and deaccessioning, and serves as a common basis for making decisions.

All of these plans need to be integrated and compatible. The collections plan will entail financial commitments—for acquisitions, storage, conservation, etc. The financial plan needs to support those commitments. The interpretive plan is probably based on the same intellectual framework as the collections plan; they are two halves of one whole and need to operate in consonance.

The collections plan must be tied closely to the museum's collections management policy, the set of board-approved guidelines that states how the museum will acquire and care for material and who has the associated authority and responsibility. The collections management policy does create some boundaries for what the museum may accession or deaccession, frequently based on such criteria as quality and completeness of title, condition, authenticity, documentation, etc. However, these criteria are mostly generic, varying very little from museum to museum. As a filter, the policy ensures that the museum will acquire or retain only material that meets certain legal and professional standards. It does not provide sufficient guidance to constitute a collections plan. Nor should it. Fundamentally different from a plan, a policy establishes general guidelines and principles that regulate the activities of the organization. It is not inherently time-limited, though it may change as museum or standards of the field evolve. Planning is the ongoing process of deciding what, specifically, the museum wants to do. The plan specifies what will be accomplished in a given period, why, by whom, and with what resources. In the case of the collections plan, the "what will be accomplished" is the acquisition or disposal of selected pieces to shape the collection, and the "why" is the intellectual framework, rationale, and assumptions that explain those choices.

Collections management policies frequently include a scope statement that describes the museum's collections. This section sometimes overlaps with the collections plan; for a more thorough discussion of this issue, see Description of the Existing Collection on page 19. Keep in mind the definition and functions of a policy versus a plan (see figure 2) when deciding how much information about the content of the collections, and in what form, to include in the collections management policy and the collections plan.

Length of the Plan

There is no "right" length for a planning document. The collections plans the authors have examined range from six to 22 pages (plus appendices). The length of your plan will depend on your museum's needs and complexity and the level of detail necessary to guide your decision-making. Keep in mind, however, that short planning documents are more likely to be widely read, used, and understood than large and unwieldy ones.

One strategy for controlling length is to create separate documents for things that can be covered in more depth elsewhere. For example, page 20 discusses the benefits of including a brief history of the collection in the plan. It might require 25 pages to do justice to the history of your 200-

year-old collections and the dozens of curators who contributed to their growth. But 25 pages of history may stop the average reader in his tracks. Consider producing a one-page version for the plan as well as a separate version that provides more detail.

Audience for the Plan

The plan may have various audiences—internal, external, staff, governing authority, etc.—and various functions. Museums sometimes create different versions tailored to fit these needs. They all say the same thing, of course, but provide different levels of detail or use different terminology to ensure they "speak the language" of the appropriate audience. All the museum's policies and plans are methods of communication, often with many people who do not already know what you know. A historian may know why labor history, for example, is important and fascinating, but he needs to convey that to a visitor or the development staff or security officer, who have less background in history.

The audience also may influence the plan's format; for example, a major donor may want a one-page "wish-list" that summarizes your acquisition priorities. The version of the plan for the museum's members, donors, journalists, etc., may be short, general, and include photos or sketches to enhance the visual appeal. Longwood Gardens, for example, publishes and sells a public version of its long-range planning document called "The Planning Vision." A version to be shared and discussed with colleagues in other museums may be much longer, more detailed, and use more technical or academic terminology.

The internal version for use by staff may be the only version that includes the action steps, budget, and timeline. This level of detail may not be needed by other users. The staff version also may include confidential information, such names of potential donors or specific targeted acquisitions, which would be inappropriate or unwise to share outside the institution.

Explain Your Reasoning

One test of whether a collections plan is effective is this mental exercise: would two different groups of people, acting independently but guided by the plan, arrive at similar decisions regarding acquisitions, deaccessions, and allocation of resources? For example, if the curatorial staff turns over two years into the implementation of your museum's five-year collections plan, will the plan enable the new curators to maintain the museum's course? To help different users of the document to interpret it consistently, include details on the rationale for its provisions. Throughout the document explain not just what the plan, or goal, or strategy is, but why those choices were made.

Flexibility

No plan is cast in stone. In implementing plans, staff must adapt to unforeseen circumstances, take advantage of serendipity, and adjust for setbacks. For example, after the Sept. 11, 2001, terrorist attacks, the National Museum of American History had to devise a method to document a whole new topic of historic importance; clearly this event was important enough to transcend existing plans. Museums also may lose what they thought would be long-term loans, and have to collect objects to fill the resulting gaps in their exhibits.

Participants in collections planning often are concerned about flexibility. There seems to be near-universal nervousness regarding the "one that may get away"—a hypothetical ur-collections object that would be a fabulous addition to the museum but may not be encompassed by the plan. Collections planning reenacts the mythic dilemma of Scylla and Charibdis: a museum can founder on the rock of inflexibility or be sucked into the whirlpool of indiscriminate collecting. In deciding how flexible to make the plan, take both of these perils into account. But pay particular attention to the fact that "flexibility" can easily become chaos. If the museum has the opportunity to acquire something so wonderful that it will transcend your plan, use the plan as a useful framework for testing that decision, to see if the object survives a hard look at your rationale, analysis of resources, etc. However, museums whose plans include the equivalent of "and we also will collect anything else that looks good" may quickly find themselves swamped by the same issues of overcrowding, unfocused collecting, or whatever reasons impelled them to engage in planning in the first place.

Elements of the Plan

Executive Summary

A primary purpose of the written collections plan is to serve as an educational tool—to bring new members of the staff and governing authority into the loop, for example, or communicate with policy makers, funders, members of the public and the press. Many of these people may never read the whole plan; an executive summary will encapsulate it for them. The summary also serves as a useful overview and orientation for readers who will proceed to study the whole document. It should be short, but since this is in proportion to the length of the entire plan, that might mean a half-page or it might mean four pages. Be guided by the question, "Will my intended audience read something this long?"

Because the summary may be the only part of the plan that is read by many people, try not to use jargon or technical vocabulary that is only explained deeper in the text. While clear, concise, jargon-free writing is always desirable, this is particularly true for the summary, which may function as the museum's sound-bite regarding its collections plan. While this is the first section in the plan, it is best to write it last.

Purpose of the Collections Plan

Never assume that everyone knows or agrees about why your museum is engaged in collections planning. It is important to establish why you are planning and the purpose of the resulting plan. Some reasons for planning might include:

- identifying the important pieces missing from the collection, so the museum can pursue them
- making decisions about how the museum can reduce the size of the collections, so that it can live within its means
- finding unifying themes to ensure that collecting is coordinated across departments and supports the museum's interpretive goals
- preparing a compelling case statement to leverage funding for acquisitions

To staff heretofore unfettered in their collecting decisions, "we need to plan what to collect" may be misinterpreted as "we want to collect less because we don't value collecting." "We need to prioritize" may be heard as "you can't have what you want." Be explicit and truthful; it may reassure people or it may confirm their worst fears, but at least it will create realistic expectations.

Values

A collections plan is a good place to affirm the museum's values regarding collecting and collections. One of the biggest impediments to collections planning (or any planning for that matter) is distrust or outright fear on the part of the staff or governing authority, who may feel threatened by the process. The planning process can affirm why and how museums value collections.

Authorship

Document how the plan was developed, who participated, who wrote it. Many of the people who will read and use the plan were not involved in creating it. At a very large museum, the planning process may not be all-inclusive. At any museum, staff may come on board after the plan is completed. New staff can help the plan evolve and adapt to changing circumstances, but you can't reinitiate the entire planning process every time the museum gets a new curator or a new registrar. The plan reflects an enduring institutional vision that should transcend the tenure of any individual. However, for it to be effective, every individual responsible for implementing the plan has to believe in it and accept its authority, which derives in large part from the authority and credibility of the people and the process that led to its creation. Curators may be reassured to know that appropriate subject-specific expertise helped develop the criteria and set priorities for acquisitions. Registrars and conservators may want to know that knowledgeable input was given regarding the resources needed to support collecting. Members of cultural groups may be more willing to donate objects or financial support if they know that their community was involved in the planning process. This is also an opportunity to honor and thank those who put countless hours into the difficult task of planning.

Outlining the process can serve several other purposes as well. People usually want to know how the final decisions were made. Was there a consensus? Did each collecting department write its own section after collaborating on the overall framework? Being explicit about the planning process helps the museum be transparent and accountable in its operations. It also helps make the next round of planning easier. If this process went well, you won't need to reinvent the wheel or search the files for a record of how it was done; it will be summarized in the plan.

Setting the Stage

As discussed on page 11, under Context, the collections plan is only one of a number of documents that guide the museum's decision-making. To help the reader understand the collections plan in the context of these other documents, some museums include:

- mission or statement of purpose
- vision statement
- overview of current strategic plan
- summary of the relationship of collections plan to other museum policy and planning documents

Sources of more information on these documents are listed in appendix E. Sample mission statements, visions statements, and strategic plans, etc., are available to AAM institutional member museums from the AAM Information Center.

Intellectual Framework (Vision for the Collections)

This is discussed at length in "Building an Intellectual Framework." The intellectual framework answers the question "where are we going?" It identifies intended audience(s) and their use of the collections and articulates the role the collections play in helping the museum fulfill its mission. This is the lynchpin of your plan; develop the intellectual framework first, and let the rest of the plan flow from there.

In the written plan, the intellectual framework may appear as a separate section, or it may be incorporated into many parts of the document—history, scope, analysis of strengths and weaknesses. There is some value in having a version of that can be read as a stand-alone piece. Because the intellectual framework provides the compelling vision of why the museum collects what it does, why that is so important and exciting, and why the museum is uniquely suited to fill this role, it is a very useful statement to present to staff, members of the governing authority, members, funders, donors, policy makers—in short, anyone you want to care about what you do.

Identifying the audience, the users of the collection, is a very important part of the framework. Any collection is useful only insofar as it meets the needs of someone—visitor, community member, researcher. Deciding what is "right" for the collection requires identifying that audience and understanding its needs. Present a compelling case that states how people's lives are affected by the collections.

Description of the Existing Collection

A plan is a roadmap, a way to navigate to a new future. To make such a map you have to know your starting point. Collections planning requires a thorough understanding of the museum's collections, why it has them, and how they compare to the collections needed to support the intellectual framework. Collections plans usually include a description of the collections, frequently in a section called "scope of collections."

Many collections management policies also contain a scope of collections statement. When AAM and the National Museum of American History prepared for the November 2002 Collections Planning Colloquium, staff examined many collections management policies to see if their scope statements could constitute a collections plan. For the most part, they did not. (See pages 12-13 for a discussion of the distinct roles of policies and plans.) Few collections management policies stated whether the scope was intended as a recitation of what the museum has, or a description of what it wants to have, or both. The scope often seems to have been written as the first, but ends up guiding decisions as if it were the second. For example, a museum has a collection of 19th-century needlework samplers and so they are described in the scope statement. Then when another sampler is offered to the museum, it may be accepted because the scope statement says that the museum collects samplers. A true plan is more than a rationalization of what the museum holds or a restatement of the status quo. It is a rational and analytical approach to building collections that meet the needs of the museum and its audience.

The description of the existing collections should be a portrait of what the museum *does* have, whether or not it wants it now. It should be comprehensive and include any and all misfits that have been buried in the back of the storage room for years because no one wanted to deal with them. Because the plan will help identify what the museum will dispose of, as well as what it will acquire, these "why in the world do we have this?" collections must be acknowledged.

History of the Collections

There are several reasons to include an encapsulated history of how the collections were formed. One reason is to capture and preserve the knowledge of your predecessors. Most museums build on the work of previous generations of staff. Understanding their choices and how and why they made them is useful context for future decisions.

Another is to acknowledge political realities. Let's be frank; material sometimes ends up in collections because it was donated by an important and influential person—a board member, a donor, or another VIP. Accepting it may have been necessary at the time, even if the material did not really fit the museum's mission or needs. Remembering why this material was accepted can help the museum assess whether it should find a better home for it or whether it must hold onto it for political reasons.

A review of the history can be particularly important for museums whose collections were shaped by one or two major donors or by the museum founder. This may be a fundamental factor in the intellectual framework that shapes collecting; the strongest influence for some museums may not be social or scientific or historic themes, but staying true to the vision of the founding collectors.

Reviewing the history of how the collections were formed also can be a way to move the process forward. One of the barriers to planning discussed in "Museum Politics" is people who are resistant to change. Explicitly acknowledging and honoring "the way things used to be" can set the stage for moving on.

Strengths and Weaknesses of the Existing Collections: Gap Analysis

Once the museum has outlined what it has and what it wants to have, it can identify what it needs to do to turn the real collection into the ideal collection. This is accomplished by comparing the existing collections to the vision of what you want the collections to be, identifying the differences (gap analysis), and setting priorities for what you want to dispose of or acquire. This takes into account practical constraints (such as museum resources) and opportunities to collaborate with other organizations.

Any comparison needs a point of reference. To determine whether an existing collection is weak or strong, staff compare it to the intellectual framework and the need each collection is trying to fill for the audiences who use it. A collection can be quite small, lacking significant depth or breadth, and still be perfectly adequate for the museum's needs if it supplements or enhances primary material. A collection can be quite large and comprehensive and still fall short if it does not meet the museum's goal to hold the preeminent collection in that area.

Each museum needs to decide what makes a collection strong or weak, and how to measure this. Strength might be gauged, for example, by:
- significance
- quality (of the object and its associated documentation)
- quantity
- completeness
- condition
- existence of ancillary collections (manuscripts, photographs, etc.)

Similarly, "weakness" might mean:
- gaps (missing material)
- lack of fit with the museum's intellectual framework and mission
- insufficient quality or significance
- inappropriate provenance
- duplication or redundancy

For each collections category, the plan should outline what the museum intends to do, which can include:
- acquiring additional material
- deaccessioning existing material
- keeping the collection as it is, neither adding nor subtracting material.

It is important to specify any of these actions, where appropriate. The collections plan is not just a plan for acquiring objects. It is equally important to clearly identify what you will get rid of and what you will not collect. All acquisitions require resources—time, money, space, conservation treatment—and the museum has limited resources. Accepting material just because it is "free" (i.e., donated) may limit the museum's ability to actively acquire and care for material it really wants. Maintaining inappropriate collections drains the museum's resources.

One very powerful thing the museum can do is place its collections in the context of other similar or complementary collections, locally, regionally, nationally, or internationally. No museum can collect everything, and it is practical to think about which organizations already collect and interpret material relevant to your mission. This is particularly germane if they serve the same audience as your museum or can lend you the material you need for exhibits. It is not necessarily productive for a museum to "compete" with other institutions for collections. A cooperative approach to planning and sharing collections may be mutually beneficial. See appendix A for examples of collections plans that incorporate this strategy.

Setting Priorities

The collections plan often prioritizes potential acquisitions and deaccessions. Because the planning process is an opportunity to look at the big picture of the museum's needs and resources, it is a good time to make these decisions This can help ensure that relatively thankless tasks like deaccessioning, which otherwise may be put off indefinitely, are brought to the front burner. It also ensures that the museum thinks strategically about what acquisitions to give preference to when allocating space, time, money, etc. Without this context, it may be hard for the group or individual making acquisition decisions to choose appropriately between item A and item B. Setting priorities also can be a valuable tool for leveraging funds or donations. It can be very persuasive to tell a donor that the desired object is the museum's top priority for acquisition, and to be able to explain why. Priorities can be influenced both by what the museum wants and by practical considerations.

Strategies

Some collections plans set strategies for collections development. A strategy outlines the general way the museum will approach any given problem, in this case, shaping the collections. For example, some museums explicitly commit to active collecting (seeking out what they want and spending the necessary resources to acquire it); some limit themselves to passive collecting (accepting what is offered to them if it meets their needs). Some museums may concentrate on building an acquisitions fund;

others may pursue a strategy of cultivating donations from owners of desired objects.

Criteria for Acquisitions or Deaccessioning

As discussed on pages 12-13, criteria for acquisitions or deaccessioning often appear in the collections management policy. Some museums repeat or amplify these criteria in their collections plans; see appendix A and AAM's forthcoming book on collections management policies (2004) for examples.

Specifics of Implementation

The above elements all establish what the museum wants to do. These goals are broad and, hopefully, enduring enough to guide the museum for five or 10 years or beyond. It may take a long time to achieve the museum's vision for the collections.

No planning process is complete, however, without:
- action steps specifying how the museum will accomplish these goals
- assignment of responsibility for these action steps
- identification of existing and needed resources (time, space, money) and how the museum will acquire them
- a timeline for implementation

These specific steps may be laid out in a section of the plan that deals with implementation; this section may be more short-range than the overall plan, covering only the next one to three years. Or each year the museum may create a detailed implementation plan that links these elements to that year's budget and work plan. For example, the current collections plan of The Children's Museum of Indianapolis covers the years 2002-2006 and is used to create detailed yearly work plans for the staff.

Evaluation

Planning, like many well-intentioned resolutions, sometimes fails due to lack of follow-through. Successful planning creates systems to review whether the museum is achieving what it intended and take correction actions, if necessary. The implementation plan should specify:
- How the museum will measure whether the plan is succeeding. On a small scale, this might be accomplishing the action steps in the imple-

mentation section. On a larger scale, it might be "peer-recognition of the excellence of our Early American collections."

- Who will perform these measurements and on what schedule.
- How the museum will use the results of this evaluation. If you are succeeding–celebrate. If the plan isn't working, why not? Are your goals unrealistic? Should you revise the strategies for implementation?

Revision and Renewal of the Plan

Planning is a continuous process. A museum engaged in successful planning is always reviewing the existing plan, making adjustments, and thinking about when the next big planning push should begin. The plan itself can assist with this by stating, for example, that the plan and its evaluation data will be reviewed periodically, specifying when (e.g., annually) and by whom (e.g., the board of trustees). ■

Figure 1: Sample Outline for a Collections Plan

Executive Summary

Preamble:

    Purpose of collections plan

    Audience for the document

    Authority: how the plan was developed, who participated, who wrote it

Setting the Stage:

    Museum mission or statement of purpose

    Museum vision

    Overview of major points of current strategic plan

    Relationship of collections plan to other museum policy and planning documents

Intellectual Framework (vision for the collection)

Analysis of Existing Collection

    Description/scope

    History

    Strengths and weaknesses: gap analysis

    Connections to other institutions and their collections

Shaping the Ideal Collection

    Priorities for acquisition and deaccessioning

    Strategies for acquisition and deaccessioning

    Criteria for acquisition and deaccessioning

Implementation Strategy

    Action steps

    Timeline

    Assignment of responsibilities

Evaluation

Reviewing the Plan

Figure 2: Policies versus Plans

POLICIES	PLANS
■ General guideline to regulate the activities of the organization ■ Standards for exercising good judgment ■ Delegates authority for implementation ■ Not inherently time-limited; endures until circumstances require change	■ Specific goals to be achieved ■ Rationale for these choices ■ How they will be achieved ■ Who will implement? ■ When it will happen? ■ What it will cost? ■ Time-limited; intended to be achieved in a finite period of time

THE PLANNING PROCESS

By Elizabeth E. Merritt

he written document is the least important part of collections planning; at best, it is a means of remembering the plan and communicating it to others. The planning process that brings that document into being and keeps it alive is far more important. The most common source of failure for any kind of planning is the lack of follow-through. A nicely bound document that sits of the shelf and is pulled out when the museum needs to demonstrate it has a plan is often the result of a process that failed to engage the energy and imaginations of the people responsible for implementation. The next chapter, "Museum Politics," discusses barriers to successful collections planning and how to overcome them; this chapter outlines the best practices and various options for any planning process. For more information on planning, see *Secrets of Institutional Planning* (forthcoming from AAM, 2004).

Characteristics of Successful Planning

Planning is most successful when it is:

- an institutional priority
- supported from the top
- nurtured with appropriate resources (time, money)
- an explicit part of the work of the governing authority and staff, on which they are evaluated and for which they are rewarded

How can you do this, given limited resources, and all the other demands on the museum's attention? It helps to remember that planning:

- is a way of conserving resources, making sure that they are not wasted on low priorities and are devoted to the most important things
- prevents emergencies, one of the great devourers of attention and resources; sometimes all that is needed to prevent a catastrophe is to realize it can happen

■ can be a way of working, rather than something in addition to your daily duties (see Integrating the Plan into the Museum's Work, at the end of this chapter)

Methods of Planning

There are as many ways to engage in successful planning as there are museums. There is no one right way. However, there may be methods that are more or less suited to your institution depending on its needs, politics, culture, and resources. Here are some parameters you might consider when selecting a planning process.

Bottom-up Planning

Bottom-up planning starts with a broad constituency—a smaller team considers and filters input from many people, arriving at a plan that is based on information from and opinions of the broad group. Some museums start with the audience, using focus groups or open meetings to gather input from their visitors. Some museums create an inclusive process that elicits input from the staff and volunteers. Such broad-based, inclusive processes tend to:

■ be realistic because they are based on input from many people with different sources of information and diverse points of view
■ help the museum move beyond "business as usual"
■ be powerful motivators for most of the staff, since they were included in the process and can see how their input shapes the results

On the other hand, bottom-up planning also can be:

■ time-consuming, especially at large institutions
■ labor-intensive to manage
■ unproductive, if the museum does not devote the time and attention necessary to keep it going

Bottom-up planning may be particularly useful at museums that want to consolidate and energize staff around a vision for the future, and large, complex institutions that must feed a variety of information and perspectives into the planning process. This approach may involve the constituencies named above—users of the collection, the museum's audience, front-line staff, educators, development staff, etc.—all of whom are affected by decisions regarding the content of the museum's collections. Or it may include just the collections-related staff—registrars, conservators, exhibit-designers, interpreters, collections managers, curators, etc. There is great value in creating a broadly inclusive planning process that includes end-users of the collection and a wide variety of museum staff. Traditionally, collections are one of the most inwardly focused areas of the museum, yet they are the heart of what most museums do. A narrow collections planning process can create a narrow vision for the collections, and, by extension, for the museum.

Top-down Planning

At some museums, top-down planning consists of the director going into his or her office, shutting the door, and writing the plan. At others, it may involve a small team comprised of top management. In either case, top-down planning is characterized by a relatively small group of people drafting a plan, which they may then give to the rest of the staff and outside stakeholders for their input or present directly to the governing authority for approval.

Top-down planning can:
■ be fast, making it suitable for responding to situations that need immediate action
■ conserve resources, using the time of relatively few people

On the other hand, top-down planning also can be:
■ constrained by limited information or a narrow vision of the future
■ alienating to staff, volunteers, and other constituents who feel excluded from the process

Top-down planning may be applicable at museums whose director's leadership style cannot embrace a more inclusive planning process; museums in crisis that need to create a plan quickly; and museums with limited resources to devote to planning.

Some museums use a combination of approaches. For example, the New York Botanical Garden (NYBG) planning process took place in three overlapping phases: (1) a mini-plan or proto-plan, created by a small group of senior staff to jump-start fund raising; (2) the program plan, created through a broadly inclusive process that gathering input from managers at every level, and (3) the master plan, which detailed the capital project costs needed to achieve the program plan goals.[1] The program planning team comprised 85 people, including 12 board members. Over the course of two years, this team listened to presentations first from front-line managers; then from the directors to whom those managers reported, who synthesized the managers' views and presented recommendations; and then from the vice-presidents, who summarized everything that had been said at that point and made their own recommendations. Director Gregory Long then synthesized those recommendations into a plan that he presented to the board for approval. NYBG may not be a "typical" museum, given its size; it has more than 350 full-time staff. But the process it used demonstrates a) that even at a large museum planning can be inclusive, and b) a museum can mix and match planning methods to take advantage of the strengths of each.

Consultants

Some museums hire consultants to help with the planning process. This assistance may range from giving advice on specific points to facilitation services to leading the process and writing the plan. Other museums successfully conduct planning entirely in-house, using only members of the staff and the governing authority.

Consultants can:
- bring an outside perspective, including knowledge of what has and has not worked at other museums
- make the best use of the staff's limited time
- provide skills, such as facilitation, that your staff may not have

On the other hand, if the process is not managed well, using consultants can lead to such drawbacks as:
- the production of a plan that does not truly represent the vision of the staff and board
- a commensurate lack of buy-in from staff and board for implementation
- missed opportunities to grapple with big and controversial issues on which members of the staff and board may disagree

None of these benefits or drawbacks are inevitable consequences of using a consultant. Each museum must decide for itself whether a consultant can improve its planning process and in what way. If you do hire a consultant, be clear about what you want him to bring to the process, what you want him to do, and who else will be involved the process and in what way.

In collections planning, consultants serving as facilitators or moderators may be particularly useful if the staff has fundamental differences of opinion about such contentious issues as:

- collecting areas the museum may freeze or discontinue
- changing long-standing traditions regarding collections or the authority to accept collections
- ethics

A neutral, outside voice may be able to help these discussions move forward productively. See "Museum Politics" for more on this topic.

Integrating Planning into the Museum's Work

Planning can be used to tie together all aspects of museum operations. As discussed in the previous chapter, no plan exists in isolation. Planning can be an opportunity to revisit a museum's mission and vision and see if they need to change. Different staff within the museum may be responsible for different parts of planning—financial, programmatic, facilities, etc. However, these planning processes must be coordinated so that the resulting plans reinforce each other rather than work at cross-purposes. In addition, planning is most effective when it is integrated into the museum's work, rather than treated as a separate, episodic activity. Some ways of achieving this include:

- Base the agendas of some board or staff meetings on the plan—reviewing progress and discussing next steps, checking the need for adjustments to the plan.
- Tie annual work plans and performance reviews to the plan, which establishes action steps, timelines, and assigns responsibility. Accomplishment of these steps can be the primary measure of staff performance.
- To facilitate planning, decide what not to do. During periods when the museum devotes a lot of time to writing or renewing the plan, con-

sciously decide what can be left undone to give staff time to devote to the planning process. Merely adding the plan to everything else the staff does won't make it a true priority.

- Build the financial plan and yearly budgets around the operational/ programmatic/ collections plans. The plan should drive the numbers, not vice versa. Any plan, even if it deals exclusively with programmatic issues, should forecast the associated financial figures, both expenses and income. Put another way, any plan should be presented in two languages: English and math.

See appendix E for some recommended resources on how to engage in planning. ■

References

1. For more information, see "Strategic Planning at the New York Botanical Garden," parts A and B, a case study produced by the Darden Graduate School of Business Administration, University of Virginia, Charlottesville.

MUSEUM POLITICS

By James B. Gardner

he collections planning process leads board and staff not only to reexamine basic assumptions about the museum's mission and its role in the community but also to challenge assumptions about traditional staff roles and areas of authority. Some people may find this energizing and exciting, but in others it may provoke anxiety or stress. Put simply, there may be strong resistance to planning from various quarters. To be successful you must deal with this resistance and get buy-in from everyone—if you aren't careful, planning may end up a casualty of museum politics.

Barriers to Planning

Each museum has its own culture, and that culture can help or hinder the kind of change inherent in collections planning. In seeking a unified vision for the collections, an institution may be challenging fundamental assumptions about museum roles and responsibilities and undermining dearly held autonomy. Since success will depend on preparing people for change and getting all stakeholders on board; the planning process is, as the previous chapter notes, more critical than the document that is produced. Managing change is not easy, but it is essential to success. In the final analysis, all must recognize that "it's not about me; it's about the museum."

That's a position, however, that may meet with resistance from staff who are accustomed to autonomy, especially if they don't trust management. When change is on the agenda, staff may suspect management's intentions and see efforts to establish a museum-wide vision or plan as restrictive rather than empowering, as negative rather than positive. The best way to overcome this distrust is to include everyone in the process and emphasize that collections planning is not just an assignment but a commitment to change.

Resistance to change may also reflect different perspectives on what is best for the museum. Most curators have personal visions of their work and the collections in their care—it is a natural effect of curator's training, professionalism, and dedication to their work. Collections planning challenges individual visions by emphasizing the primary importance of an institutional vision. Also, when you are so focused on the objects themselves, it's hard to step back and think about collecting from a thematic or conceptual perspective. We often are so committed to existing collections that we are unwilling to consider new directions or look beyond to the longer term. And there are real, practical concerns about stewardship responsibilities; it's fine to talk about collecting across departments, but who receives the objects and is responsible for their management and care?

The situation is exponentially worse for large institutions that not only face individual staff resistance but may have an organizational structure in which staff identify more with their separate collections departments than with the museum. Unless skillfully handled, the museum's plan can end up as simply a sum of the parts rather than a holistic vision.

Senior management can present challenges as well. From their perspective, collections planning may seem like an intellectual enterprise, of limited practical importance to the museum. Demonstrating how planning can be used to leverage resources puts planning in a larger context of responsible management. Getting buy-in from your governing authority can be a bit trickier. It is vital to involve them, but there are practical limitations to having them too deeply involved. Consider the planning process as an educational activity, a way of helping them to understand collecting and generate excitement about new collecting opportunities. When members of the governing authority start talking about what the museum should collect rather than their own individual interests, you'll know you've been successful.

Using the Process to Break Down Barriers

How you organize the process can make all the difference in the success of your planning. The leadership team is critical. You need individuals with content expertise and knowledge of your institution and who are engaged individually and collectively; good group dynamics is essential.

And that means making sure that everyone speaks the same language and that planning doesn't get derailed by misunderstandings and miscommunication.

Since planning of this sort can be scary for some staff, it may make more sense to approach it in segments. Start with a manageable and realistic agenda. A planning process that is long and drawn out and has nothing to show for the first year can result in skepticism, resistance and indifference. Indeed, that was a concern of the collections planning steering committee at the National Museum of American History, which initially organized its work around drafting four pieces of the plan:

- a preamble that would set the stage for the plan
- an intellectual framework
- an analysis of the existing collections, including a survey of connections to other institutions and their collections and a comparison of existing collections to the intellectual framework
- an implementation strategy

The time frames were different for each, and the focus was on what was doable in the short run. The first piece was particularly important; it addressed why the museum was developing an institutional collections plan, what its goals were, and how it would be developed. This "preamble" working group was charged to expedite its work so that the draft could be circulated right away to help staff get a better sense of what was going on and how it would affect their work. The "intellectual framework" working group had the longest time frame since it had the most difficult task. And the "collections assessment" group could do only preliminary baseline work until there was a consensus about the intellectual framework, against which the collections would be assessed. But perhaps the most important working group was the one charged with developing implementation strategies; it looked for existing collecting models that could be the basis for "quick wins," concrete demonstrations of how collecting could be changed. Those early successes would in turn provide the foundation for implementing the larger museum-wide plan. Demonstrating the potential of planning for changing the way the museum works can go a long way in generating credibility for the process and undercutting the collective eye-roll that can doom an initiative as "more planning for the sake of planning."

It's a good idea to disseminate your work in draft form; don't present the end product as a done deal, developed and imposed from above or outside. Share progress on at least a monthly basis and ask for feedback from stakeholders; everyone should be involved all along the way. To facilitate discussion, explore alternative formats. For example, a group of documents accessible through a shared folder, with links to reference and other materials, will convey a better sense of a work in progress than a single document handed out in hard copy for review. This also can foster perception of the plan as dynamic, not static. Keep in mind, too, that the same documents may not work for all; you may want a conventional document for your governing authority, a fluid one for staff, and something more concise for the public and other external stakeholders.

Implementing Your Plan

It is one thing to write a plan, it is quite another to implement it; indeed, that is where most planning fails. With luck and skill, the planning process will be accepted by your staff, but it is possible that indifference and even outright resistance will remain.

Implementation begins with the language and tone of the plan itself. If your plan is fuzzy, unrealistic, or just a wish list, it isn't going to lead to real change. The plan needs to articulate a compelling argument and demonstrate real benefits to the museum and its stakeholders. And it must identify practical strategies that will lead to success; consider identifying three goals or strategies that will be the museum's immediate priorities.

But even the most carefully crafted plan is useless if you cannot change behavior. You do not want your planning fossilized in a document that sits ignored on the shelf. So how do you change the way people are used to doing business? One thing you can do is to demonstrate how the plan helps people get what they want. Almost all collections staff want more resources—space, time, money—to better care for and develop the collections. When deaccessioning frees up space and generates acquisition funds, or when donors offer to give the priority items on your acquisition list because they are swayed by your compelling vision of the collections, that is powerful, positive feedback and will win over the skeptical and build support.

While that may motivate some staff, you should not assume that that will be enough. To make your new collections plan real, you must embed it in the museum's work by making its implementation a priority in individual staff performance evaluation. In other words, you must hold staff accountable.

In the final analysis, you may find that some staff simply won't agree with the planning efforts or the museum's change in direction. They may have deep intellectual disagreements with the choices made. They may find their value system clashes with the process you create. Or they may find the new way of doing business is simply not one that makes them happy in their work. In such a situation, you really have only one course of action left: develop graceful exit strategies so that those staff members can leave with dignity.

But the work doesn't end with implementation. How do you ensure that the planning process is worth the effort? A critical element is evaluation. To assess the process, you must establish measures or benchmarks that will document success and provide a basis for next steps. How do you keep the plan alive and relevant to the work of the museum? Collections planning must be an ongoing process. Establish a process of regular review and revision that will provide for continual shaping and refining of the plan and the collections. This in turn provides a great motivator for staff, providing positive feedback and an opportunity to acknowledge their successes. When you have gone through a full cycle of planning, implementation, and evaluation, you will probably find that many of the barriers you faced have fallen, as people see for themselves the benefits of the process.

Collections planning won't be easy, and you'll face many obstacles. But few museums can afford to continue with business as usual; our choices about what to collect and not collect must be better informed. That doesn't mean that collections planning should be seen as a burden; rather it should be embraced as an important opportunity to refocus the museum and re-engage the staff, to move collecting from routine to energized. ■

THE AUTHORS

James B. Gardner is associate director for curatorial affairs, National Museum of American History, Smithsonian Institution. Previously he worked as a consultant with museums and higher education and also served as deputy executive director of the American Historical Association and as director of education and special programs for the American Association for State and Local History (AASLH). His professional activities include service as president of the National Council on Public History and chair of the Nominating Board of the Organization of American Historians, AASLH Nominating Committee, and AASLH Committee on Standards and Ethics. His publications include *Public History: Essays from the Field* (1999), *Documenting the Digital Age* (1997), *Ordinary People and Everyday Life: Perspectives on the New Social History* (1983), and contributions to *The Public Historian, Museum News*, and other periodicals.

Elizabeth E. Merritt, director of Museum Advancement and Excellence at AAM, has 15 years experience in museums, including administration, curation, and collections management. Before joining AAM in 1999, she was director, collections and research, at Cincinnati Museum Center, responsible for the administration of the curation, collections management, research, and conservation efforts related to the natural history and science, history, and children's museums of the Center. Her areas of expertise include collections management and planning and museum assessment. She has served as member-at-large and chair of the Education and Training and Membership Committees of the Society for the Preservation of Natural History Collections (SPNHC); a General Operation Support reviewer for the Institute of Museum and Library Services; and as liaison from AAM and SPNHC to the AAM Registrars Committee. ∎

SAMPLE SECTIONS FROM COLLECTIONS PLANS

This appendix presents excerpts from collections plans created by a wide variety of museums. Where possible, sections are quoted in their entirety; however, sometimes only an illustrative segment is used. Not every museum names or arranges sections in the same manner; these examples are arranged to correspond with the elements presented in "Writing the Collections Plan." Complete copies of sample collections plans are available to AAM institutional member museums from the AAM Information Center. *Note:* copyright in the excerpts listed here is held by the respective institutions.

These excerpts illustrate the manner in which different museums tackle these issues. No one example can or should be used as a substitute for your own original collections plan. Your museum, its needs, and its values are unique, and you should tailor your plan accordingly. In addition, much of the value of planning comes from the process of discussing, weighing options, debating values, and coming to decisions. Relying too heavily on sample plans as models can shortchange your museum.

Executive Summary

See page 56 for The Children's Museum of Indianapolis's executive summary.

Purpose of the Plan

Chesapeake Bay Maritime Museum Collections Plan, revised Dec. 14, 2001

This plan will guide the Chesapeake Bay Maritime Museum in fulfilling the part of its mission to collect and preserve the maritime history of the tidewater Chesapeake Bay region by setting criteria for items that are appropriate to its collections. It outlines areas for growth and refinement of existing collections. This plan also supplements the museum's Collections Policy (updated and adopted in 1993) by elaborating on and clarifying the museum's scope of collections. The museum's interpretive themes (outlined in section 1.B.2) define what collections the museum will aggressively seek, where we will concentrate staff energies and acquisition budgets; the scope of collections (section II) will guide decisions about the limits of collections that we will accept if offered.

Purpose of the Plan and Authorship

Collecting Plan of the State Historical Society of Iowa, 1993

This collecting plan was created by the Society's Collections Committee, representing the Society's bureaus, board of trustees, and the public. The collecting plan defines, coordinates, and integrates the collecting efforts of the State Historical Society of Iowa. Staff, space, and funds for collecting are limited; the Society cannot collect everything, nor should everything be collected. By articulating the following recommendations, assumptions, guidelines, and areas of special emphasis, this collecting plan provides the framework within which staff can make daily collecting decisions on an individual or bureau level. The intent of this plan is not to dictate, but to guide collecting decisions so that collections development at the Society will benefit from coordinated and integrated collecting objectives.

This collecting plan is a first step. Of greater importance are processing and analysis of collections, and sharing that information, which will further refine the Society's collecting efforts.

Values

Cincinnati Museum Center Anthropology Department Archaeological Collection Plan, draft, Feb. 12, 1999

It is the acquisition and long-term curation of meaningful and information-rich collections that distinguishes museums from all other kinds of research and educational institutions.

The Children's Museum of Indianapolis 2002-2006 Collections Plan, April 2002.

Objects are powerful storytellers that elicit emotional responses that can connect generations.

The Mariners' Museum Collections Philosophy

The core asset of any museum is its collection. From this collection the museum derives its identity, its strength, and ultimately, its product.

Setting the Stage

Cincinnati Museum Center Anthropology Department Archaeological Collections Plan, draft, Feb. 12, 1999

Mission of the Anthropology Department

The Anthropology Department furthers scientific and historical knowledge and understanding of past human societies of the Eastern Woodlands with a focus on the rich archaeological legacy of the central Ohio River valley. The Department acquires and preserves scientifically and historically significant collections of well-documented artifacts and preserves the archaeological record for the benefit of research scholars and the public. The Department conducts original research to develop new knowledge of the archaeological record and of past human societies. The Department disseminates knowledge through scholarly publications, presentations, and exhibits that describe and interpret the archaeological record.

Policy on the Use of Non-native Plants, Morris Arboretum of the University of Pennsylvania, March 15, 2000

Horticultural Mission of the Morris Arboretum

The Arboretum's horticultural mission includes growing a diversity of north temperate plants from around the world within the context of an historical landscape. Inherent to this mission, the goals of the Arboretum include continued plant exploration and collecting in the United States, Asia, and Europe. Our position as a leader in plant collecting allows us to serve as a germplasm repository for threatened species, for example *Eucommia ulmoides*. A further goal of plant exploration and evaluation is the introduction of plants with horticultural merit into the nursery trade, with an emphasis on plants selected for tolerance to urban growing conditions. Additional goals are to: 1) gain status as a national collection for selected genera, which include American, Asian, and European species, and 2) establish field trials for evaluation of superior insect and disease resistant species, such as *Tsuga chinensis*.

While the Arboretum serves as a repository for species of wild-collected and documented origin, as stewards of 165 acres of land along the Wissahickon Creek in southeastern Pennsylvania, we are responsible for preventing any unnecessary invasion of natural areas along this riparian corridor. We must be cautious in our collections policy and serve as a leader in demonstrating responsible management of a diverse collection of non-native plants. Opportunities exist to serve as a testing ground to monitor potential invasives and also to merge the Arboretum's goals of plant exploration, evaluation, and introduction. In doing so, we can enhance the horticultural diversity of the Delaware Valley while avoiding negative impacts on local ecosystems.

Intellectual Framework

The Portland Museum of Art Acquisitions Plan, January 1997

Theory of the Collection

The Museum's mission is "to improve and enrich the lives of diverse audiences and serve as a vital cultural center for greater Portland, the State of Maine, and New England." The collection carries out this mission by being the only art collection in the country to show the remarkable history of art in Maine and its connections to national and international art movements; for example, our Winslow Homers demonstrate some of the best art ever created in Maine set in the context of the Barbizon School and Realism. We seek out the best artists associated with Maine. We collect their work and complementary 18th-, 19th- and 20th-century American art as well as complementary 19th- and 20th-century European art.

Our collection provides a definitive repository of works associated with a Golden Age of art in Portland, from 1820 to 1920, represented by artists such as Benjamin Paul Akers, Harrison Bird Brown, Charles Codman, Charles Octavius Cole, and Charles Frederick Kimball.

The collection defines and promotes Maine's best art colonies including Ogunquit, Monhegan, Skowhegan, Vinalhaven, and the Cranberry Isles. We provide permanent collections that document the achievements of these colonies for future generations.

Selected areas of excellence will be collected if the works provide a critical mass of appreciation and the works are also of national and international stature. One example is the world-class works in the Payson, Black, Huntington, and Otten Collections that relate to Impressionism. Another example is the Museum's glass collection, which goes well beyond Portland Glass of the 1860s to encompass a broad overview of the glassmaker's art in America and Europe from ca. 1750-1900.

Further, the Museum, as appropriate, collects two- and three-dimensional objects that are primarily of significance to the history of Portland and the state.

Finally, the Federal-era McLellan House (1800-01) establishes a design context for the Museum's decorative arts collection related to Portland's Golden Age.

Chesapeake Bay Maritime Museum Collections Plan, revised Dec. 14, 2001

Themes:
The collections support the museum's primary interpretive themes, including:

- The essence of the Chesapeake Bay story is found in the *connections between nature and people* over time. It is the story of how this unique natural environment—America's most productive estuary—has affected individual lives and communities, as well as regional and national history.

- *People and the Bay*: From early settlement to today, the natural environment of the Bay has attracted a diverse population that has given shape to distinctive settlement patterns, communities, and cultures.

- *The Bay as an economic resource*: The Bay's productivity has provided profitable employment for people and added greatly to the diversity of maritime activity on the Bay. With this diversity comes conflict over resource use and management. Maritime enterprises have shaped the society, culture, and economy of the Chesapeake.

- *The Bay as a place of recreation*: Beginning in the mid-19th century, the Bay has been transformed into a place offering endless opportunities for recreation. The increase in recreational activities often creates cultural and environmental challenges as competition for resource use increases.

- *Trade*: the role of the Chesapeake Bay is the history of American trade. Maritime trade and exchange is a vessel of cultural transmission—the movement of not only people and goods, but ideas as well.

The Museum will aggressively seek collections that support these themes through associations with rich stories of Chesapeake people, institutions, events, and places. Staff time and acquisition funds will be devoted to pursuing collections that support these themes.

Scope and History of the Collection

Draft Collecting Plan, Kalamazoo Valley Museum, November 2001

History of Collections

The Museum's collections date from an 1881 donation of rocks and fossil specimens accepted by the Kalamazoo Board of Education as "the beginning of a new museum." The collections have now grown to approximately 46,000 artifacts, documents, and images associated with local and regional history. They play an integral role in supporting the Museum's mission through their inclusion in permanent and temporary exhibitions as well as in public programs. In addition to the permanent collection, the Museum maintains a teaching collection, available for programmatic use.

The Museum's collections represent a cultural history of southwest Michigan. Two prominent local collectors and philanthropists, Albert M. Todd and Donald O. Boudeman, devoted their energies to securing a local museum in 1927 and bequeathed their collections to insure its establishment. Their artifacts remain among the most recognized and best-loved in the collection. Other early donations reflected what members of the community felt were important enough to preserve in the community museum. This resulted in an eclectic collection that the Museum staff has refined over the last fifteen years in keeping with current museum professional standards.

Minnesota Museum of American Art Collection Development Plan, July 20, 2000

History of the Collection

The St. Paul Gallery and School of Art began a teaching collection in the early 1940s to support classroom instruction. Early donations included European furniture, works by Minnesota artists, and Asian art. As the Museum grew, it continued to collect fine and decorative art from around the world. During the 1950s through the 1970s, the Museum made purchase awards from its national juried exhibitions of drawings and studio crafts, enhancing the scope of the American collection and the institution's local and national reputation.

By the early 1980s, the Museum had assembled a collection of works from America, Europe, Asia, Africa, New Guinea, and other countries. As part of an analysis of the collection, the Museum hired scholars to examine the collection and recommend a direction for sustained growth and identity. Because of their reports, the Museum adopted a focus on American art of the first half of the century, with a special emphasis on Minnesota art, acknowledging the Museum's long-standing support of the art of the state. This allowed the Museum to develop a collection and exhibition program meaningful to area audiences and not extensively duplicated by other area museums.

The 1980s were growth years for the American collection, because of this decision, with an active program of deaccessioning many decorative arts and other marginal material and purchasing several important paintings. In 1987, a deaccessioned pastel by Edgar Degas sold at auction for $1,092,500. Proceeds were used to establish the Katharine G. Ordway Fund that allowed the Museum to begin a purchase program for the collection. Between 1983-85, the Museum also developed a comprehensive, professional collection policy and a long-range plan for the collection, including a wish list of artists with the goal of compiling a survey of American art history.

Strengths & Weaknesses of the Existing Collections, Gap Analysis

Collecting Plan of the State Historical Society of Iowa, 1993

Military Affairs

Definition and relevance of subject area to Iowa history:

Materials about homefront activities and about the experiences of Iowans during war time will be collected in order to document how wars have affected the tenor of life in Iowa, especially in the 20th century. Significant gaps exist in the Society's documentation of all 20th-century wars and conflicts (especially post-1945) and their impact on Iowa.

The Civil War continues to appeal to many of our audiences—museum visitors, researchers, readers, genealogists. Although our Civil War diaries and letters help illuminate the typical soldier's experiences, as well as complement Adjutant General regimental records, significant gaps exist regarding the average person's experience in the Civil War—whether in the military or on the homefront. For example, we have many more formal portraits of officers than candid images of camp life; we have presentation swords but not common weapons or battlefield uniforms. Homefront material regarding women's and children's roles is minimal.

The Spanish American War is adequately represented by photographs of camp life in Florida and of soldiers in the Philippines—though less so by manuscript sources.

Strengths:

- Annie Wittenmyer Collection (documents Iowa's sanitary agent's coordination of women's relief work during and after the Civil War).
- Formal portraits of Civil War officers (housed in Des Moines).
- Grenville Dodge Collection (Civil War general).
- Grand Army of the Republic photograph collection. This extensive collection of group photos of reunions and encampments (1870s-1920s) largely provides genealogical information (housed in Des Moines).
- World War I uniforms.
- Photographs of the 42nd or Rainbow Division in World War I, mostly of regiments or European settings (housed in Des Moines).

- U.S. Food Administration Collection for World War I (housed in Iowa City).

- Poster Collection (1,500 for World War I, and 2,500 for World War II).

- Casualty files for World War I and II, including a photograph and brief biography for Iowa casualties (housed in Des Moines).

- Clippings file for World War II and the Korean War (topically arranged; in need of preservation and improved access).

- Records of early militia units, including National Guard through 1914.

- Research records on Fort Des Moines Provisional Army Officer Training School, which served as a training camp for African-American officers in World War I and WACS in World War II. The records are housed in the Society's Historic Preservation Bureau.

Gaps:

- 20th-century weapons, uniforms, and equipment.

- Materials that document the impact of war on farming, business, and domestic life in Iowa.

- Women's roles.

- Objects relating to state militia units and National Guard.

- Refugees and resettlement.

- Protest movements and peace activism.

- Veterans' organizations.

- Homefront activities related to the war effort.

- Iowa's military camps (including those for African-American officers, WACS, and prisoners-of-war).

Complimentary collections at other Iowa institutions:

- Camp Dodge holds the Adjutant General's records after 1914; grave registrations for all veterans buried in Iowa; and state bonus records for war service.

- University of Northern Iowa Library: material related to student training company (1892-1900 and 1917-1918), and armed services training detachment of WAVES and Army Air Corps during World War II. Also ROTC records.

Recommendations:

National media will continue to document wars overseas; to avoid overlap and to control growth, Society collections should focus on defining the Iowa experience in wars, especially on the homefront. And to complement official records held elsewhere, the Society should seek the typical soldier's personal and everyday materials (such as photographs, letters and diaries, field uniforms, gear, and typical weapons).

The Collections Committee alerts Society staff to the timeliness of documenting Iowans' involvement on the homefront in the 20th century. Some potential interviewees are now age 70 or older; active collecting and oral history interviews need to be launched immediately. Documenting post-1945 wars also need not wait.

Cincinnati Museum Center Anthropology Department Archaeological Collections Plan, draft, Feb. 12, 1999

Collections Strengths and the Identification of Significant "Gaps"

As a research and educational institution, it is in the Museum's interest to identify both its collections strengths and weaknesses as those impinge on the Museum's ability to meet the needs of both its internal and external users.

Excavated Site Collections. Archaeological collections from well-excavated sites tend to combine the properties of representing complete assemblages of behaviorally associated artifacts and ecofacts with the most complete documentation of depositional contexts and spatial association among artifacts and ecofacts. Such collections have great research value. Table 2 lists the archaeological sites for which we have significant excavated collections.

One of the greatest strengths of the Museum's archaeological collections lies [in] its extensive suite of excavated late prehistoric sites. Ten excavated site collections cover the entire temporal range of the late prehistoric cultures (A.D. 1000-1625) in central Ohio River valley. Some of these late prehistoric site assemblages have received a great deal of research attention (see Table 1).

Much less well represented by excavated samples are the earlier periods of tri-state prehistory. Small assemblages from six archaeological sites represent the Late Woodland period (A.D. 450-1000), and although southwestern Ohio is world-famous for its Hopewellian Middle Woodland sites (A.D. 1-450), this period is represented in the Museum's collections only by excavations at two Hopewell earthworks sites and one Middle Woodland mound. Early Woodland components (1000 B.C.-A.D. 1) are limited to three sites, all mortuary deposits. The 7,000-year-long Archaic period (8000-1000 B.C.) is particularly poorly represented with only a single site yielding good context Archaic artifacts, and the collections lack excavated samples for the Paleoindian period (prior to 8000 B.C.). The Museum's excavated collections do not include truly representative samples of American Indian site contexts for any of these important periods of regional prehistory nor for the contact period (ca. A.D. 1650-1780).

Nineteenth-century urban historical archaeology is well represented by strong collections from the Betts Longworth Historic District in downtown Cincinnati, which produced well over 50,000 items from well-dated privy excavations. A much smaller artifact sample of 19th-century urban artifacts comes from test excavations of privy contexts at Findlay Market. The region's small-town 19th-century life is currently represented only by artifacts from limited test excavations at the Parker House site in Ripley, Ohio.

Major gaps in the Museum's holdings for local historical archaeology include assemblages representing the region's rural communities, military sites (including important late 18th-century and Civil War-era sites); local/regional 19th-century industrial sites, such as ceramic and glass-production sites; site assemblages from 19th-century African-American residences and businesses; and assemblages representing the initial Euroamerican settlement of the region in the late 18th century through early 19th century.

Setting Priorities

The Children's Museum of Indianapolis 2002-2006 Collections Plan

Acquisitions

The major acquisition goal for the Natural Science collection will continue to be Cretaceous dinosaurs, eggs, and supporting contextual materials. The greatest upcoming "real specimen" use will be in "Dinosphere" (2004), where the number of dinosaurs and related materials on display will place us within the top five museums in the country for "real bone" on exhibit. Additional Natural Science upgrades will occur in the areas of mammalogy, petrology, mineralogy, and paleobotany (2002-ongoing) to benefit natural science work throughout TCM.

Minnesota Museum of American Art, Collection Development Plan, July 20, 2000

Areas of No Recommended Growth

Objects of primarily historical or cultural importance do not form a significant aspect of the collection. As the Museum's collections have developed, collecting for historic or cultural significance has not been a priority, rather attention is focused on aesthetic quality as the basis for acquisition consideration. As such, objects of material culture including toys, tools, musical instruments, historic documents, and many items of furniture are not collected.

Other areas of minimal or no holdings include: industrial or graphic design and architectural design. None of these areas is recommended for development within the collection unless a remarkable collecting opportunity presents itself. Objects in areas not recommended for growth should be carefully reviewed for deaccession.

Strategies

The Children's Museum of Indianapolis, Five-Year Plan Highlights 2002-2006, Acquisitions

Convert long-standing loans to gifts.

Establish individual or corporate donors to support specific types of collections acquisitions. Remove inappropriate, poor condition, unusable, duplicate, or potentially hazardous materials from all collection areas.

Colorado Historical Society Collection Plan, 2004-2008

Implementation Strategy

The Colorado Historical Society's Collection Plan develops and strengthens the Society's collections by guiding Society staff, Board, and the general public in the acquisition and preservation of artifacts and archival materials for research, interpretation, and exhibition. The plan strengthens the Society's ties to Colorado communities and provides an opportunity for community building through collections. The plan upholds professional museum and archival standards and provides the Society's individual curatorial departments with institutional guidelines that aid in the formulation of the respective departmental collecting strategies.

Implementation of the Collection Plan requires that we identify objectives and strategies to meet these goals.

Objective: Develop the collection through proactive collecting that:
- targets growth areas,
- fills significant gaps, whether typological, geographic, demographic, or chronological,
- anticipates future research or programmatic needs.

Strategy:
- Survey and evaluate current collections to identify and assess strengths and weaknesses.
- Seek funding for surveys, purchases, and collection maintenance.

Objective: Maintain the integrity of the collection by accepting or retaining only those items that:
- have strong provenance,
- are in good condition or endowed with sufficient funds to conserve or restore them,
- fulfill a specific need (documentation of community groups, public issues, exhibit, research, etc.),
- may be properly documented, stored, and maintained.

Strategy:

- Develop a standard Acquisition Proposal form.
- Present potential acquisitions at regularly held Staff Collections Committee meetings.
- Seek additional funding for proper documentation, storage, maintenance, and conservation of collections.

Objective: Broaden the Society's presence throughout the state by:

- working with communities to determine how our collections can best serve them,
- acting as a state, regional, and national resource through collaborative community projects.

Strategy:

- Partner with advisory councils and community groups to build relationships.
- Survey county, city, and local history museums to determine where their collection strengths may complement ours.
- Act as a clearinghouse by referring potential donors to other more appropriate museums.
- Seek funding to develop and implement community projects

Objective: Refine the collection by divesting of items that:

- do not fulfill the Society's mission,
- have suffered such significant deterioration that they cannot be restored,
- are unusable due to damage too costly to repair,
- are duplicates,
- have no provenance,
- cannot be properly stored and maintained.

Strategy:

- Survey, identify, and recommend the deaccession and disposition of artifacts in accordance with Society procedures.
- Seek funding for deaccession implementation.

Criteria for Accessioning/Deaccessioning

The Mariners' Museum, Collection Philosophy

Criteria for Selection:

- Historical significance
- Relevance to existing collections
- Uniqueness
- Importance of the artist or producer
- Condition and preservation needs
- Format or size

The Museum of International Folk Art

General Guidelines for Acceptance of New Acquisitions:

Condition: MOIFA seeks objects that are in good condition or that can reasonably benefit from conservation treatment. Those objects that require extensive treatment will be accepted only after careful consideration and when funding will be sought for their treatment.

Use: Additions to the collection will be made only after consideration has been given to future use in terms of documentation, research, and exhibition. Objects for which there is not a clear justification of need or suitability will not be accepted. Some items may be acquired as non-accessioned objects to serve an educational function.

Storage: MOIFA realizes the need to balance the growth and development of future collections with the care and maintenance of the present collections. All decisions regarding gifts, loans and purchases must take into consideration the finite storage facilities available at MOIFA and any special requirements for their preservation. Acquisition by the museum pre-supposes a long-term financial commitment by the State of New Mexico for proper curation and conservation. Accordingly, those items or collections presenting special problems or conditions of care will be subject to careful review prior to acceptance into the collection."

Implementation

Policy on the Use of Non-native Plants, Morris Arboretum of the University of Pennsylvania, March 15, 2000

Implementation of this policy will be the primary responsibility of the Director of Horticulture. A committee also representing the Botany and Public Programs Departments shall participate in annual evaluation of the progress and effectiveness of the program. Monitoring the collection and determining which plants should be added or removed from the target list will be done by the Horticulture and Botany staffs.

Executive Summary

The Children's Museum of Indianapolis 2002-2006 Collections Plan

Executive Summary

One enduring reason visitors have for returning to The Children's Museum is to share and remember with others the "things" they experienced as children. The essence of visitors' memories is the tangible objects at TCM—the carousel, the polar bear, the water clock—and those "landmarks" guide people's physical orientation within the museum space.

It is our responsibility to collect, manage, and use artifacts and specimens that fulfill TCM's mission of creating "extraordinary learning experiences that have the power to transform the lives of children and families." Artifacts inspire imagination, offer insight, and are valuable reference points for families, who use them to compare their lives to the lives of others, across time and cultures. The diversity of our 100,000-plus cultural and natural objects allows us to address almost any theme. If the most-often asked visitor question is, "Is it real?" we can say, "Yes, it is."

Objects are powerful storytellers that elicit emotional responses that can connect generations. They take on their own lives in the contexts of exhibits and programs. Objects become meaningful teaching and communication tools that reach far beyond the physical constraints of the museum proper. That idea, combined with technological possibilities, gives a virtual dimension to the collection that has never existed before.

Artifact/Specimen Use: Over the next five years, the Collections Department will continue to increase its artifact and specimen use while moving into new areas of digitization and image access. In March 2002, we converted to a new collections management software (KE Emu), used by other institutions such as the Minnesota Historical Society, the Museum of Science and Industry, and the Smithsonian. This new software enables us to capture, manage, and share object images and information, things we were unable to do in the past. We are presently scanning older photographic images into the database, as our budget allows, and changing old records into newly accessible ones.

Starting in 2002, all acquisitions will have digital images. We are working with InfoZone to reference the "top 100" curator-designated museum specimens and objects on the InfoZone Web site by July; these will also be on the Museum's Web site. We will supply images and information to this ongoing project (pending funding and staffing), utilizing all permanent collection museum objects.

Primary and continuing object use is in a support and supplementary capacity for temporary, traveling, and permanent exhibits and for education and programmatic use. We intend to grow object use from nearly 5,000 yearly to 10,000-15,000 by 2006. In 2001 we began our first accurate tracking of the number of artifacts used each quarter. This number fluctuates greatly depending upon the number of exhibits requiring supplementary artifacts; the rotation of objects into new or revised galleries; or the number of loaned objects going out that year. The use number also varies, according to the types of hands-on education or program opportunities available.

Traditionally at TCM, exhibits and programs have been idea-driven rather than artifact-driven. In 2003, TCM launched our first in-house large temporary exhibit driven by our strong collection of puppets. As part of a larger Exhibits plan to "look inward" to our artifacts for exhibits, we are taking some exhibit rental fees and using those funds to create our own exhibits. This is a giant step forward to ensuring greater application of our artifact resources. By 2006, at least three TCM temporary exhibits will have resulted from the strength of our collections.

Acquisitions: The major acquisition goal for the Natural Science collection will continue to be Cretaceous dinosaurs, eggs, and supporting contextual materials. The greatest upcoming "real specimen" use will be in "Dinosphere" (2004), where the number of dinosaurs and related materials on display will place us within the top five museums in the country for "real bone" on exhibit. Additional Natural Science upgrades will occur in the areas of mammalogy, petrology, mineralogy, and paleobotany (2002-ongoing) to benefit natural science work throughout TCM.

Another example of artifacts acting as a catalyst for exhibit development is the upcoming permanent exhibit, "The Power of Children," inspired by TCM's 2001 acquisition of the Ryan White Collection from the White family. The exhibit, paired with objects and stories about Anne Frank and Ruby Bridges, will feature contents of Ryan's 1980s bedroom and present a familiar context that encourages families to share thoughts about prejudice and consider the actions they might take to make a difference in the world.

Year-to-year collecting plans will be aligned with exhibit development, upgrades, revisions, and themed education and programmatic endeavors. For the American Collections, this includes the acquisition of television-related materials ; the addition of an iconic American object—a Harley Davidson motorcycle—for the Harley Davidson temporary exhibit (2003); music, visual arts, and popular culture items for the redo of the older American galleries; and the *Chihuly Kaleidoscope* (pending funding) glass sculpture for the core. As with the dinosaur acquisitions for "Dinosphere," the acquisition of what will be the world's largest permanent Chihuly sculpture will bring national and international attention to TCM's cultural collections.

In the World Cultures area, the redo of the Passports gallery into a new Global Perspectives gallery (possibly in 2008) will dictate upcoming acquisition goals, with Africa as the first gallery focus. Subsequent gallery changeouts will similarly influence collecting plans. World culture artifacts will play a prominent role in any What If? gallery revisions after 2006.

Additionally, we hope to convert several long-term loans (2002-03) to donations, including the mummy Wenehotep and the 1930s Parry Family Collection of Native American materials. We continue to grow the Caplan

Collection through yearly "folk/ fantasy/play" artifact acquisitions and will be increasing access and use of that collection once cataloguing is completed in 2006. The management of the Caplan Collection will be greatly enhanced once information is available in our database.

Our present acquisitions budget for the three collecting areas (American, World Cultures, and Natural Science) stands at $75,000 but needs to grow to a minimum of $100,000 per year to enable us to be competitive in the museum field. While we obtain some objects through donation, we rely on purchasing abilities to address specific collecting needs. By 2004, we hope to connect with corporate and individual donors who could support collections acquisition.

Deaccessions: Part of the management plan for the Caplan Collection includes removal of unaccessioned, inappropriate, poor-condition, or duplicate items through auction, with dollars returning to support the collection. We also may have to deaccession some Caplan pieces from the permanent collection.

Deaccessioning should never be thought of as the best answer for increasing acquisition dollars or creating additional storage space. It should be considered a necessity for the viability, consistency, and proper management of the collections and for ensuring that they remain relevant to the museum's mission and visitors. The amount of time, research, and paperwork required to dispose of an object from the collection can be twice that required to bring an object into the collection. This underscores the importance of properly aligning collection plans with yearly institutional priorities.

Disposing of an artifact or specimen may occur through a sale to a dealer; a sale or donation to another museum or related institution; an auction; by reassigning it to TCM Education Resource (hands-on) use; or by destroying it, if it's dangerous or in a state that can't be repaired. At least 80% of the objects deaccessioned in the past 10 years were given an assigned curatorial outgoing value of less than $100. Many sold at auction realized less than $30. Deaccessioning is an ongoing process for each collecting area. Maximum return of dollars into the Collections Acquisition fund probably peaked at around $50,000 several times in the mid-1990s, with the sale of stockpiled American collections including extraneous train materials, dolls, and a coverlet collection.

We are continuing to deal with artifacts and specimens that came into the collection over 70 years ago that are less relevant to TCM's present mission and strategic plan. This includes many 19th-century American farm tools, furniture and pioneer artifacts, World Cultures' Casas Grandes pottery, weaponry, poor quality textiles and other items, and duplicates, as well as materials that would be better suited to other museums or historical organizations within Indiana or elsewhere. As collections are honed, by 2005 deaccessioning should decrease within the American and Natural Science collections and gradually increase in World Cultures. As much as 8 to 10% (or 10,000 items) of the collections total could be tagged for deaccessioning in the next 10 years if the Museum chooses not to develop exhibits around the impressive textile collection or utilize the immense Caplan Collection or the growing 20th-century popular culture collection.

Storage/Conservation: While deaccessioning creates space for useful incoming artifacts, that "found space" is soon consumed through storage upgrades to appropriate archival quality boxes and reshelving to create adequate space and address environmental needs. Our deaccessioning rate cannot always keep pace with our rate of acquisition; incoming artifacts stored properly also consume space. Our percentage of used objects is high but to prolong their lives, objects also need "resting" space.

In coming years, major acquisitions of dinosaurs, additional toy collections, and possibly larger cultural materials will push our storage capabilities to the brink. In 2004 the Museum must address a plan for expansion or off-site storage. Present leakage problems in lower collections storage must be corrected in 2003. To properly maintain the collection, lab upgrades will be needed by 2005. Ultimate collections management may come after 2006 when we begin to test using barcodes to track the collections.

Conclusion: In 2001, as a component of staff training, the Collections Department articulated a mission statement that emphasizes our commitment to obtaining, using, and maintaining "diverse collections that influence, educate, and inspire children and families." As institutional beliefs and practices regarding the collections change, more artifact-driven exhibits will surface. Additional collections-based exhibits will begin to exist in "virtual space" (2004-onward). Increased use of objects will place greater demand on artifact and specimen conservation repair and cleaning needs, appropriate mounts, exhibit environments, research time, data entry, digital imaging, and movement tracking. Fiscal and personnel support issues will grow along with our new initiatives. Currently, there are 12 staff in the Collections Department who commit their talents, skills, and time toward making extraordinary experiences come to life with extraordinary artifacts and specimens. ■

DISCUSSION SUMMARIES FROM THE NATIONAL COLLECTIONS PLANNING COLLOQUIUM

hese summaries encapsulate the discussions of 20 staff from the National Museum of American History, 61 staff from 36 other U.S. institutions, and 10 facilitators at the Nov. 15-16, 2002, National Collections Planning Colloquium. (See appendix G for a list of participants.) The colloquium was designed by AAM staff and presented with support from the National Museum of American History.

Collections Planning: Characteristics of an Intellectual Framework

An intellectual framework for collections is:

1. Grounded in the museum's mission. The mission by itself is usually too broad to guide collecting. The intellectual framework is more specific; this helps focus collection goals.

2. Built around the needs of the end users. Who are the audiences? Will they use collections for research, exhibits, programming?

3. A starting point for the museum's strategic plan in all areas of museum activity (collections plan, public programs, research plan, interpretive plan, exhibits, etc.).

4. An effective bridge between the mission and the collections, explaining why the collections are important, how they support the museum's ability to fulfill its mission.

5. An eloquent explanation of why the museum collects what it collects, why the collections are emotionally compelling, how they form a coherent whole.

6. Often organized around interpretive themes that may guide exhibits and programming as well as collecting.

7. An expression of the vision of the institution, not of an individual or one segment of the staff.
8. Flexible enough to adapt to changing circumstances.
9. Firm enough to guide decision-making.
10. Helpful in determining when there is "enough" in a given category, based on a clear understanding of need—what are the collections for, and what is sufficient (or excessive) to meet that need?
11. At some point, reconciled with available resources; what can you acquire and care for given resource constraints?
12. Necessary for integrating the activities of different collecting departments in the museum (including library, archives) as well as exhibits, education, etc.

Collections Planning: Strategies for Planning and Implementation

Common barriers to successful collections planning and implementation:
1. Lack of context (mission, vision, strategic plan)
2. Lack of time to plan
3. Scarcity of resources (staff, space, money)
4. Gaps in institutional knowledge regarding collections contents, significance, history
5. Gaps in staff knowledge, lack of key subject area expertise
6. Resistance to change, lack of buy-in, fear of loss of autonomy
7. Lack of commitment on part of leadership
8. Institutional culture, size of staff, barriers between departments
9. Cynicism regarding planning, particularly if past efforts have failed

Strategies for successful collections planning and implementation:
1. Start with a reassessment of institutional mission and vision, if this is needed.
2. Make collections planning an institutional priority, part of the strategic plan.
3. Ensure leadership (board and director) send clear message that collections planning is important.
4. Commit the resources (time, responsibility, money) needed for success.

5. Clearly articulate the expected benefits from planning, for example:
   a. Commitment and ability to leverage needed resources for collections care and development (donations, funding)
   b. Tool for deflecting unwanted acquisitions
   c. Measure of accountability, a way for the museum's collections component to define and demonstrate success
   d. Cost savings (and therefore more resources for collections)
   e. Improved ability to fulfill mission
   f. Improved organizational stability and financial health
6. Clearly articulate negative consequences of "not planning"
7. Continued or growing lack of resources (time, space, money)
8. Loss of institutional direction and history
9. Inability to control unwanted collecting
10. Unwillingness of board to devote resources to collections if there are no measures for accountability
11. Expense of maintaining collections people don't want and don't need, and lack of tools needed for deaccessioning
12. Negative impact on financial health of museum and therefore its ability to care for and support collections
13. Failure to "be all the museum can be" and fulfill the mission
14. Start with a thorough understanding of the museum's collections, of their significance, and the quality (good or poor) of their current care.
15. Analyze staff expertise and identify areas where you may need outside experts.
16. Work on the intellectual framework/vision/themes early on in the process. It is a necessary foundation for planning.
17. Create specific assignments, responsibilities, deadlines for completion. Include these in annual work plans and performance evaluations.
18. Encourage participants to see the big picture; this is not just the creation of a wish list.
19. Be broadly inclusive in the planning process; include board, administration, staff, and outside stakeholders.
20. Build trust through clear lines of communication.
21. Be honest about potential outcomes (e.g., the museum may stop collecting in some areas or may make changes in staffing).

22. Use outside facilitator to mediate sensitive discussions. Give people "safe" opportunities to vent fears and frustrations, engage in blue-sky thinking.
23. Specify clear, achievable goals in the plan.
24. Value and respect input from all staff, recognize the expertise each brings to the process.
25. Be clear that in the end the plan serves the needs of the institution, not individuals.
26. If necessary, create graceful exit strategies for people who cannot buy in to the process. ■

ACCESSING SAMPLE DOCUMENTS FROM THE AAM INFORMATION CENTER

The AAM Information Center is building a collection of sample documents from all types and sizes of museums. Sample documents are available as a benefit of membership only to institutional-member museums.

The following types of sample documents are currently available. To help the Information Center staff select documents that best fit your needs, please note your museum's discipline, budget range, and governance structure in your e-mail request. Contact: infocenter@ aam-us.org.

- Bylaws for museums and support organizations
- Codes of Ethics
- Collection Plans
- Collections Management Agreements (an agreement between 2 organizations through which one provides curatorial services for collections owned by the other)
- Collections Management Policies
- Conservation Plans
- Copyright and Reproduction Policies
- Delegation of Authority (documentation of authority & responsibility delegated by the governing authority to the museum director)
- Disaster/Emergency Plans
- Facility Use Agreements

- Governance Transition Plans (documents related to a change in governance structure, such as from municipal to nonprofit)
- Institutional Plans
- Management Agreements (an agreement between 2 organizations detailing roles & responsibilities of each)
- Mission Statements
- Mothballing Historic Structures Materials
- Organization Charts
- Performance Appraisal Forms
- Personnel Policies
- Position Descriptions
- Statements of Permanence (for museums with a non-museum parent organization: evidence of the museum's existence and permanence)

Please note: the *Standard Facility Report* is not available as a sample document but can be purchased from the AAM Bookstore. ∎

APPENDIX D

GLOSSARY

Benchmark: a standard or point of reference used to measure and/or judge quality or value.

Collecting plan: plan that identifies what the museum wants to acquire over a period of time. Colloquium participants believe this is distinct from a *collections* plan (see below), which also considers deaccessioning, resource allocation, partnerships with other museums, and other aspects of building and sustaining the collections.

Collections management policy: a written document, approved by the governing authority, that specifies the museum's policies concerning all collections-related issues, including accessioning, documentation, storage, and disposition. Policies are general guidelines that regulate the activities of the organization. They provide standards for exercising good judgment.

Collections plan: a plan that guides the content of the collections and leads staff in a coordinated and uniform direction over time to refine and expand the value of the collections in a predetermined way. Plans are time-limited and identify specific goals to be achieved. They also provide a rationale for those choices and specify how they will be achieved, who will implement the plan, when it will happen, and what it will cost.

Collections planning: the process of developing the content of a collections plan.

Deaccessioning: the process of legally removing accessioned objects from the museum's collection. Deaccessioning does not affect the museum's ownership of an object, but it does mean that the museum no longer holds the object in the public trust.

Disposal: the method by which a museum divests itself of deaccessioned material. Methods of disposal include donation, sale, trade, destruction.

Financial plan: a plan that outlines goals and strategies for income and expenditures. It may identify the museum's assets, liabilities, tolerance for risk, and strategies for income generation. The financial plan projects cash-flow needs and makes sure that the museum will have the financial resources it needs to implement its strategic plan.

Governing authority: the executive body to which the director reports and is responsible; it is charged with the fiduciary responsibility for the museum and for approving museum policy. *Names of governing authority* include: Advisory Council, Board of Commissioners, Board of Directors, Board of Managers, Board of Regents, Board of Trustees, City Council, Commission.

Intellectual control: knowledge of the collections of sufficient breadth and depth to ensure both full access to individual objects and a coherent grasp of the whole. Includes documentation of the significance, provenance, and ownership status of collections.

Intellectual framework: the underlying conceptual structure that focuses the museum's collecting efforts. Built around the mission and the needs of the users and often organized around ideas, concepts, stories, or interpretive themes that guide exhibits, programming, research, and collecting. Specific enough to guide decision-making.

Inventory: an itemized listing of the objects, often including current location, for which the museum has responsibility.

Loans: the temporary transfer of collection objects from or to the museum for stated purposes. The transfers do not involve a change of ownership.

Mission statement: a statement that articulates the fundamental reasons why the museum exists. It is used to guide the museum's operations.

Physical control (of collections): sufficient knowledge of the content, location, and condition of collections to ensure that they can be managed effectively.

Scope of collections (synonym: scope statement):
a) A description of the museum's existing collections, often categorized by object type, topic, time period, geographical boundary, or collections department.
b) A description of what the museum does collect or intends to collect. Differs from an intellectual framework in that it usually categorizes objects by type, topic, time period, geographical boundary, or collections department—rarely by ideas, concepts, stories, or themes—and does not explain why the museum has made these collecting decisions.
c) A combination of a and b.

Strategic plan (synonyms: institutional plan, long-range plan): a comprehensive plan that drives the "big picture" of the organization's future goals and activities, and covers all major areas of operation.

Synoptic collection: a "one of everything" collection developed to give an overall or general view of a topic; collection does not represent depth or variation but does document variety. (ref: *MuseumWise*, compiled and edited by Paisley S. Cato, Julia Golden, and Suzanne B. McClaren, Society for the Preservation of Natural History Collections, 2003.)

Taxonomic collection: a collection developed and organized by categories of specimens; while most often applied to animals and plants (e.g., phylum, class, order, family, genus, species), the term also is used to describe historical and other systematically developed and organized collections.

Vision statement: a compelling description of what the organization will look like, ideally, in the future. It should be challenging, innovative, and forward-looking. ■

RESOURCES

Resources on Collections Planning:

Available from the AAM Information Center[1]: sample collections plans from museums of various disciplines, governance types, and budget sizes.

Resources on Planning in General:

Collections planning is most effective when it is integrated into the museum's overall planning process.

Available from the AAM Information Center: sample strategic/institutional/long-range plans from museums of various disciplines, governance types, and budget sizes.

Creating and Implementing Your Strategic Plan: A Workbook for Public and Nonprofit Organizations, 2d ed., John M. Bryson and Farnum K. Alston. Jossey-Bass, 1995. An updated companion to *Strategic Planning for Public and Nonprofit Organizations.*

Secrets of Institutional Planning, AAM Professional Education Series, 2004 (forthcoming).

Strategic Planning Workbook for Nonprofit Organizations, rev. ed., Bryan W. Barry. Amherst H. Wilder Foundation, 1997.

Strategic Planning for Public and Nonprofit Organizations: A Guide to Strengthening and Sustaining Organizational Achievement, rev. ed., John M. Bryson. Jossey-Bass, 1995.

Resources on Collections Stewardship

Collections planning is part of a museum's overall stewardship responsibilities and should be aligned with management, preservation, and legal issues.

Available from the AAM Information Center: sample collections management policies and conservation plans.

AAM Accreditation Commission's Expectations Regarding Collections Stewardship, AAM 2001. This statement outlines why the Accreditation Commission considers collections stewardship to be important and how it assesses whether a museum is fulfilling its stewardship responsibilities. See appendix F; also available from the AAM Web site at www.aam-us.org.

AAM's Museum Assessment Program: Collections Management Assessment. MAP is a confidential, consultative process designed to help museums understand whether they reflect standards and best practices in the museum field as well as how other institutions deal with similar challenges. Participating museums engage in directed self-study, and receive a visit and written report from a peer reviewer. This assessment focuses on collections policies, planning, access, documentation, and collections care within the context of a museum's total operations. Grants from the Institute of Museum and Library Services can underwrite most of the costs of an assessment. For more information, go to www.aam-us.org.

Collections Management Policies, John Simmons. AAM, 2004 (forthcoming). Collections plans must be created in alignment with the museum's collections management policies, and those management policies need to support the collections plans. This comprehensive volume covers all aspects of developing and implementing a collections management policy.

A Deaccession Reader, edited and introduced by Stephen E. Weil. AAM, 1997. Collections planning includes comparing a museum's collections to a vision of the ideal collection. This often leads to the identification of material that should be deaccessioned to better serve the museum's mission and vision. This volume includes collections disposal policies from several museums as well as statements from professional organizations, including AAM, Association of Art Museum Directors, and American Association for State and Local History.

A Legal Primer on Managing Museum Collections, 2d. ed., Marie C. Malaro. Smithsonian Institution Press, 1998. Collections planning is founded on the museum's legal obligations to the collections in its care. This definitive reference work focuses on collections-related problems and legal-entanglement issues, reviews relevant cases and court decisions, and gives advice on when a museum should seek legal counsel.

Preservation Planning: Guidelines for Writing a Long-Range Plan, Sherelyn Ogden. AAM/NEDC, 1998. Collections planning takes into account the conservation needs of the existing collections and of the collections the museum intends to acquire. This publication guides users in writing long-range preservation plans for collections care.

Resources on Community Engagement
It is increasingly common for museums to involve their communities in their planning efforts. In collections planning, community members can give input on the needs and expectations of the community. This also can help the museum build relationships that may lead to collecting and loan opportunities.

AAM's Museum Assessment Program: Public Dimension Assessment. For a general description of MAP, see the listing under collections stewardship resources. The Public Dimension Assessment can help museums increase attendance, reach out to new audiences, or change the institution's image in the community. It helps museums get input from their community and audiences regarding what they want from the museum, how they view the museum, and how the museum can improve its service to them.

A Museum & Community Toolkit. AAM, 2002. Designed to help museums plan successful museum-community dialogues. Includes helpful hints, logistical tips, and sample documents for organizing a structured and creative conversation among people involved in the day-to-day business of building community. A companion to *Mastering Civic Engagement: A Challenge to Museums.*

Mastering Civic Engagement: A Challenge to Museums. AAM, 2002. Museum professionals offer advice on the complex process of changing the relationship between communities and museums.

Resources on Interpretation

The intellectual framework a museum creates to guide its collections development frequently also serves as the basis for its interpretive plan. In some museums, interpretive goals drive collections planning.

Exemplary Interpretation: Seminar Sourcebook, Victoria Garvin, ed. AAM, 2001. Prepared for the 2001 AAM Professional Educational Seminar on Interpretation, *Exemplary Interpretation* contains institutional self-assessment tools used in the National Interpretation Project, sample documents and examples of best practices, perspectives on interpretation from five AAM Standing Professional Committees, principles of experience design, and a checklist on the essentials of great interpretation.

Interpreting Historic House Museums, Jessica Foy Donnelly, ed. AltaMira Press/American Association for State and Local History, 2002. In historic house museums, collections plans are frequently tied to furnishing plans and interpretive plans. The book's 14 contributors address the need to consider familiar issues from new perspectives and using new methods.

Notes

1. The AAM Information Center provides online resources for all AAM members. The resources in the members-only section of the AAM Web site (www.aam-us.org) provide guidance on museum operations, standards and best practices, and emerging issues. In addition, the Information Center offers reference services to institutional member museums, including access to a growing collection of sample documents. ■

AAM ACCREDITATION COMMISSION'S EXPECTATIONS REGARDING COLLECTIONS STEWARDSHIP

Approved June 27, 2001

The Accreditation Commission's expectations reflect the evolving nature of standards and practices in museums. During its review of over 100 institutions a year, the Commission discusses how current practices in museums relate to the existing *Criteria and Characteristics of an Accreditable Museum*. Often, after thorough deliberation, the Commission re-articulates its expectations. The Accreditation Office periodically issues and updates documents like this one to keep the museum community informed.

Why does the commission consider collections stewardship important?

Stewardship is the careful, sound, and responsible management of that which is entrusted to your care. Possession of collections incurs legal, social, and ethical obligations to provide proper physical storage, management, and care for the collections and associated documentation, as well as proper intellectual control. Collections* are held in trust for the public and made accessible for the public's benefit. Effective collections stewardship ensures that the objects the museum owns, borrows, holds in its custody, and/or uses are available and accessible to present and future generations. A museum's collections are an important means of advancing its mission and serving the public.

(*See definitions at the end of this document.)

What are the Accreditation Commission's expectations regarding collections stewardship?

Per Program Eligibility Criteria:

- An accredited museum, either collecting or non-collecting, is required to have a formal and appropriate program of documentation, care*, and use of collections and/or tangible objects.*

- An institution that owns collections (including living organisms), whether actively collecting or not, it is required to have accessioned* at least 80 percent of its permanent collection.*

Per the *Characteristics of an Accreditable Museum*, an accreditable museum must demonstrate that its:

- collections and/or tangible objects are appropriate for its mission

- collections and/or tangible objects are effectively managed, housed, secured, documented, and conserved

- public programs, collections, and exhibitions effectively advance the mission

The commission also expects an institution to:

- plan strategically and act ethically with respect to collections stewardship matters

- legally, ethically, and responsibly acquire, manage, and dispose of collection items, know what collections are in their ownership/custody, where they came from, why they have them, and their current condition and location

- provide regular and reasonable access to, and use of, the collections/objects in its custody

- balance the good of the public and the good of the collections

This requires thorough understanding of collections stewardship issues to ensure thoughtful and responsible planning and decision-making. With this in mind, the Commission emphasizes systematic development and regular review of policies, procedures, practices, and plans for the goals, activities, and needs of the collection.

How does the commission assess whether the institution's collections and/or tangible objects are appropriate for its mission?

The commission compares the institution's mission—how it formally defines its unique identity and purpose, and its understanding of its role and responsibility to the public—to two things:

- the collections and/or tangible objects used by institution

- its policies, procedures, and practices regarding the development and use of collections and/or tangible objects.

(See also the *Accreditation Commission's Expectations Regarding Institutional Mission Statements*.)

In its review, the Commission expects:

- the mission statement is clear enough to guide collections stewardship decisions

- the collections owned by the museum, and objects loaned and exhibited at the museum, fall within the scope of the stated mission

- the mission, scope of collections statement in the collections management policy, and other collections-stewardship-related policies are in alignment and practiced.

How does the commission assess whether the institution effectively manages, houses, secures, documents, and conserves its collections and/or tangible objects?

The Commission recognizes that there are different ways to manage, house, secure, document, and conserve collections, depending on their media and use, the museum's own discipline, size, physical facilities, geographic location, and financial and human resources. Therefore, the Commission considers many facets of an institution's operation which taken together demonstrate the effectiveness of its collections stewardship policies, procedures, and practices. The Commission considers the museum's collections stewardship policies, procedures, and practices in light of these varying factors.

The Commission also recognizes that museums may have diverse types of collections categorized by different levels of purpose and use—permanent, educational, archival, research, study, to name a few—which may have different management and care needs. The Commission expects these distinctions to be articulated in collections-stewardship-related policies and procedures.

The Commission also recognizes that different museum disciplines may have different collections stewardship practices, issues, and needs related to that specific field. The Accreditation Commission expects museums to follow the standards and best practices appropriate to their respective discipline and/or museum type as applicable.

In its review, the Commission expects:

- a current, approved, comprehensive collections management policy is in effect and actively used to guide the museum's stewardship of its collections
- 80 percent of the permanent collection is formally accessioned and an appropriate and reasonable percentage of the permanent collection is cataloged, inventoried, and visually documented
- the human resources are sufficient and the staff have the appropriate education, training, and experience to fulfill the museum's stewardship responsibilities and the needs of the collections
- staff are delegated responsibility to carry out the collections management policy
- a system of documentation, records management, and inventory is in effect to describe each object and its acquisition (permanent or temporary), current condition and location, and movement into, out of, and within the museum
- the museum regularly monitors environmental conditions and takes pro-active measures to mitigate the effects of ultraviolet light, fluctuations in temperature and humidity, air pollution, damage, pests, and natural disasters on collection objects
- an appropriate method for identifying needs and determining priorities for conservation/care is in place
- safety and security procedures and plans for collections and objects in the museum's custody are documented, practiced, and addressed in the museum's emergency/disaster preparedness plan

- regular assessment of, and planning for, collection needs (development, conservation, risk management, etc.) takes place, and sufficient financial and human resources are allocated for collections stewardship

- the storage space (on and off-site) is adequate in terms of size, condition, use, access, and security

- collections care policies and procedures for objects on exhibition, in storage, on loan, and during travel are appropriate, adequate, and documented

- the scope of a museum's collections stewardship extends to both the physical and intellectual control of its property

- ethical considerations of collections stewardship are incorporated into the appropriate museum policies and procedures

- considerations regarding future collecting activities are incorporated into institutional plans and other appropriate policy documents

Does your museum need help with collections stewardship?

Free information from AAM (all available at www.aam-us.org)

- *Code of Ethics For Museums*, American Association of Museums, 2000. (A brochure format is also available through the AAM Bookstore, see below).

- *AAM Guidelines on Exhibiting Borrowed Objects*, 2001

- *AAM Guidelines Concerning Unlawful Appropriation of Objects During the Nazi Era*, 2001

Free information from the AAM Accreditation Program (202/289-9116; accreditation@aam-us.org; www.aam-us.org/accred.htm)

- *Accreditation Commission's Expectations Regarding Institutional Codes of Ethics*

- *Accreditation Commission's Expectations Regarding Institutional Mission Statements*

- *Accreditation Commission's Expectations Regarding Institutional Planning*

Definitions (from the *Accreditation Self-Study*, 1997)

Collections: Objects both animate and inanimate that have intrinsic value to science, history, art, or culture. Collections reflect, in both scope and significance, the museum's stated purpose.

Tangible objects: Materials used to communicate and motivate learning and instruments for carrying out the museum's stated purpose.

Care: The museum keeps appropriate and adequate records pertaining to the provenance, identification, and location of the museum's holdings and applies current professionally accepted methods to their security and the minimization of damage and deterioration.

Permanent collections: Those that are of intrinsic value to art, history, science, or culture and that support the mission of the museum and are held and curated by the museum.

Accessioning: The creation of an immediate, brief, and permanent record utilizing a control number for an object or group of objects added to the collection from the same source at the same time, and for which the museum has custody, right, or title. Customarily, an accession record includes, among other data, the accession number; date and nature of acquisition (gift, excavation, expedition, purchase, bequest, etc.); source; brief identification and description; condition; provenance; value; and name of staff member recording the accession. ■

LIST OF COLLOQUIUM PARTICIPANTS

Anchorage Museum of History and Art, Anchorage, Alaska
Municipal Governance; Accredited
Representing the museum: Walter Van Horn, Curator of Collections

Ashland, The Henry Clay Estate, Lexington, Ky.
Private Nonprofit Governance
Representing the museum: Eric Brooks, Curator

Carnegie Museum of Art, Pittsburgh
Private Nonprofit Governance; Accredited
Representing the museum: Sarah Nichols, Chief Curator and Curator of
    Decorative Arts

Chesapeake Bay Maritime Museum, St. Michaels, Md.
Private Nonprofit Governance; Accredited
Representing the museum: Pete Lesher, Chief Curator

Chicago Historical Society
Private Nonprofit Governance; Accredited
Representing the museum: Alison Eisendrath, Senior Collection Manager,
    and Kathleen Sam Plourd, Director of Collections Services

The Children's Museum of Indianapolis
Private Nonprofit Governance; Accredited
Representing the museum: Sheila Riley, Director of Collections

Colorado Historical Society, Denver
State Governance; Accredited
Representing the museum: Bridget Burke, Curator of Books and
    Manuscripts, and Moya Hansen, Curator of Fine and Decorative Arts

Fenton History Center–Museum & Library, Jamestown, N.Y.
Private Nonprofit Governance
Representing the museum: Claire Davis, Trustee, and Christin Stein,
    Director

Historic St. Mary's City, St. Mary's City, Md.
State Governance; Accredited
Representing the museum: Silas Hurry, Curator of Collections and
    Archaeology, and Martin Sullivan, Executive Director

Japanese American National Museum, Los Angeles
Private Nonprofit Governance; Accredited
Representing the museum: Karin Higa, Director of Curatorial and
    Exhibitions, and Cris Paschild, Archivist and Manager

Kalamazoo Valley Museum, Kalamazoo, Mich.
College/University Governance; Accredited
Representing the museum: Patrick Norris, Director

Loudoun Museum, Leesburg, Va.
Private Nonprofit Governance
Representing the museum: Randy Davis, Curator, and Christie Hubner,
    Collections Manager

Lowe Art Museum, University of Miami, Coral Gables, Fla.
College/University Governance; Accredited
Representing the museum: Brian Dursum, Director and Chief Curator

Lower East Side Tenement Museum, New York
Private Nonprofit Governance
Representing the museum: Stephen Long, Curator, and Natalie Moran,
    Collections Manager

Mariners' Museum, Newport News, Va.
Private Nonprofit Governance; Accredited
Representing the museum: Susan Berg, Vice President/Director of the
    Library

Maryland Historical Society, Baltimore
Private Nonprofit Governance; Accredited
Representing the museum: Nancy Davis, Deputy Director, and Jeannine
    Disviscour, Curator

Michigan State University Museum, East Lansing
College/University Governance; Accredited
Representing the museum: Laura Abraczinskas, Collections Manager for
    Natural History, and Lynne Swanson, Collections Manager for
    Cultural Collections

Milwaukee Public Museum
Private Nonprofit Governance; Accredited
Representing the museum: Alex Barker, Curator and Chair,
    Anthropology, and Randy Mooi, Curator of Fishes

Minnesota Historical Society, St. Paul
Private Nonprofit Governance; Accredited
Representing the museum: Marcia Anderson, Chief Curator, Museum
    Collections, and James Fogarty, Head, Acquisitions and Curatorial
    Department

Monterey County Agricultural & Rural Life, King City, Calif.
County Governance
Representing the museum: Meg Clovis, Cultural Affairs Manager, and
    Joy Malis-Hey, Collections Manager

Museum of Fine Arts, Museum of New Mexico, Santa Fe
State Governance; Accredited
Representing the museum: Aline Brandauer, Assistant Director for Long-
    Range Planning, and Christine Mather, Curator of Collections

Museum of Texas Tech University, Lubbock, Texas
College/University Governance; Accredited
Representing the museum: Eileen Johnson, Curator of Anthropology, and
   Nicola Ladkin, Registrar

Mystic Seaport, Mystic, Conn.
Private Nonprofit Governance; Accredited
Representing the museum: William Cogar, Vice President, Collections &
   Research, and Douglas Teeson, President

National Cowboy and Western Heritage Museum, Oklahoma City
Private Nonprofit Governance; Accredited
Representing the museum: Melissa Owens, Registrar, and Chuck Rand,
   Research Center Director

National Museum of American History, Smithsonian Institution,
   Washington, D.C.
Trust instrumentality of the Federal Government; Accredited
Representing the museum:
   Joan Boudreau, Asst. Chair, Division of Information Technology and
      Society
   Jeanne Benas, Registrar
   Shelly Foote, Asst. Chair, Division of Social History
   Karen Garlick, Asst. Director, Dept. of Coll. Management Services
   Patricia Gossel, Chair, Division of Science, Medicine, and Society
   Peter Liebhold, Museum Specialist, History of Technology
   Carlene Stephens, Curator, Division of History of Techology
   Ann Seeger, Asst. Chair, Division of Science, Medicine and Society
   Debbie Warner, Curator, Science, Medicine and Society
   Deborara Richardson, Asst. Chair, Archives Center
   Helena Wright, Curator, Information Technology & Society
   Bill Yeingst, Museum Specialist, Social History
   Ray Kondratas, Curator, Science, Medicine, and Society
   Susan Myers, Chair, Division of Social History
   Rayna Green, Chair, Division of Social History
   David Allison, Chair, Division of Information Technology and Society
   John Fleckner, Chair, Archives Center
   Stacey Kluck, Asst. Chair, Division of Cultural History

Jennifer L. Jones, Asst. Chair, Division of History of Technology
Paula Johnson, Curator, History of Technology
Craig Orr, Archivist, Archives Center

National Museum of Racing and Hall of Fame, Saratoga Springs, N.Y.
Private Nonprofit Governance
Representing the museum: Lori Fisher, Curator of Collections

Nebraska State Historical Society, Lincoln
State Governance; Accredited
Representing the museum: Deborah Arenz, Senior Museum Curator, and
Laura Barrs Mooney, Museum Registrar

New Hampshire Historical Society, Concord
Private Nonprofit Governance; Accredited
Representing the museum: Janet Deranian, Director of Collections &
Exhibitions, and David Smolen, Special Collections Librarian

New Jersey Historical Society, Newark
Private Nonprofit Governance
Representing the museum: Janet Rassweiler, Director for Programs and
Collections, and Ellen Snyder-Grenier, Deputy Director for Special
Projects

New York Botanical Garden, Bronx
Private Nonprofit Governance; Accredited
Representing the museum: Dennis Stevenson, Vice President for Botanical
Science, and Kim Tripp, Vice President for Horticulture & Living

North Carolina Museum of Art, Raleigh
State Governance; Accredited
Representing the museum: John Coffey, Deputy Director of Collections
and Programs

Northwest Museum of Arts & Culture, Spokane, Wash.
State Governance; Accredited
Representing the museum: Marsha Rooney, Curator of History, and Laura
Thayer, Curator of Collections

Portland Museum of Art, Portland, Maine
Private Nonprofit Governance; Accredited
Representing the museum: Susan Danly, Curator of Graphics,
    Photography, and Contemporary Art; Jessica Nicoll, Chief Curator and
    William E. and Helen E. Thon Curator of American Art

Rogers Historical Museum, Rogers, Ark.
Municipal Governance; Accredited
Representing the museum: Marie Demeroukas, Curator of Collections

Tallahassee Museum of History and Natural, Fla.
Private Nonprofit Governance; Accredited
Representing the museum: Linda Deaton, Curator of Collections and
    Exhibits, and Mike Jones, Curator of Animals

The Wolfsonian–FIU, Miami, Fla.
College/University Governance; Accredited
Representing the museum: Marianne Lamonaca, Assistant Director, and
    Frank Luca, Associate Librarian

Witte Museum, San Antonio, Tex.
Private Nonprofit Governance; Accredited
Representing the museum: Marise McDermott, Vice President for
    Planning and Research, and Elisa Phelps, Director of Collections

Discussion Facilitators:
Patricia Ainslie, Vice President, Collections, Glenbow Museum, Calgary,
    Alberta, Canada
Rebecca A. Buck, Registrar, Newark Museum, N.J.
Christine Flanagan, Director of Public Programs, United States Botanic
    Garden, Washington, D.C.
Victoria Garvin, Assistant Director, Professional Education, AAM
Judy A. Greenberg, Director, The Kreeger Museum, Washington, D.C.
Melissa Marsh Heaver, Registrar, Fire Museum of Maryland, Lutherville
Jane MacKnight, Registrar, Cincinnati Museum Center
Stephen E. Patrick, Director, City of Bowie Museums, Md.
Lynne Poirier-Wilson, Special Projects Curator, Asheville Art Museum,
    Asheville, N.C.

Katherine P. Spiess, Assistant Director, Strategic Initiatives, National Museum of American History, Washington, D.C.

William G. Tompkins, National Collections Coordinator, National Collections Program, Smithsonian Institution, Washington, D.C.

Conducting the Colloquium:

Jim Gardner, Associate Director for Curatorial Affairs, National Museum of American History, Washington, D.C.

Victoria Garvin, Assistant Director, Professional Education, AAM

Elizabeth Merritt, Director, Museum Advancement & Excellence, AAM

Note:

"Accredited" refers to accreditation by the American Association of Museums and reflects the museum's status at the time of the colloquium. ■

A